CW01151321

The Atari® ST™ User's Guide

John Heilborn

Osborne **McGraw-Hill**
Berkeley, California

Osborne **McGraw-Hill**
2600 Tenth Street
Berkeley, California 94710
U.S.A.

For information on translations and book distributors outside of the U.S.A., please write to Osborne **McGraw-Hill** at the above address.

A complete list of trademarks appears on page 209.

The Atari® ST™ User's Guide

1234567890 DODO 89876

ISBN 0-07-881185-6

Cynthia Hudson, Acquisitions Editor
Jean Stein, Senior Editor
Elizabeth Fisher, Editorial Assistant
Lyn Cordell, Project Editor
Yashi Okita, Cover Design

To the newest Heilborns, Leah and Magda.
We all have a lot to be proud of.

Contents

ACKNOWLEDGMENTS

When I was attending a hardware design course in Boston some years ago, one of the instructors had a sign on his desk that said: "The difficult we do immediately—the impossible takes a bit longer." I want to thank the following people at the "new" Atari for giving new meaning to that sign:

Leonard Tramiel, who introduced me to the 520-ST and always "took care of everything."

Richard Frick, Neil Harris, and Arnold Waldstein, who always knew in which direction to "point" me in an ever-changing Atari.

John Feagans, Dave Staugas, Craig Suko, Jose Valdes, and David Duberman, whose technical expertise helped make both the 520-ST and this book a reality.

I would also like to thank the following people:

My wife Sharon, who assembled (and on several occasions, produced) the illustrations, figures, and listings.

Bob Girola and Neil Armentrout of Quality Micro Systems, for providing a laser printer that would interface with the 520-ST (all of the listings and a number of the figures and illustrations were produced using the QMS Smartwriter).

Dan Williams of Home Computing Centers, who helped produce many of the illustrations at the beginning of the book.

And finally, my editors, Cindy Hudson and Paul Hoffman, for their editorial guidance in completing this book.

Introduction

Until recently, computers were often difficult to understand and occasionally cumbersome to use. Although great efforts were made to make computers easier to use, most attempts were destined to fail—until the introduction of the mouse-and-desktop type computer systems.

The Atari 520-ST is the newest of these new computers, and like its predecessors, it includes a mouse and a high-resolution video display. The ST also offers both color text and graphics, a full-size typewriter-type keyboard, ten programmable function keys, cursor control keys, and a numeric keypad. In addition, the ST has more than half a million bytes of internal memory.

Chapter 1 explains how to unpack and set up the 520-ST and its accessories. It contains a description of all the controls on the ST, from the connectors to the mouse.

Chapter 2 guides you through the ST desktop, introduces you to icons, pointers, windows, and menus, and shows you how to customize your ST to fit your needs. In this chapter you will also look at the different kinds of peripherals (such as printers and disk drives) that are available for the ST.

Chapter 3 is an introduction to the LOGO programming language, which is provided with the ST. All of the basic LOGO commands are discussed, and you are introduced to the concept of programming.

Chapter 4's topic is advanced programming techniques. It includes several practical applications of the concepts covered in Chapter 3. You will learn how to create interactive screen programs, access the printer, and save to the disk. This chapter also looks at a number of techniques for using the special program-debugging tools available in LOGO.

Chapter 5 is a tutorial on programming with the mouse and the keyboard, and it will show you how to include these two different input devices in your programs.

Chapter 6 covers graphics. It explains how the video display works, how the ST produces colors, and how you can mix characters with text. You will learn some of the fundamentals of animation, as well as creating your own special graphics patterns and shapes.

Chapter 7 is a glossary of all the LOGO statements and functions. It contains descriptions and short examples of every LOGO command.

The appendixes contain tables on all other details discussed in the text, from editing commands to error messages.

CHAPTER

Getting Started 1

When you unpack the Atari 520-ST, you will find the equipment shown in Figure 1-1. This equipment consists of

- The 520-ST computer
- A 500K floppy disk drive
- A video display (either RGB color or high-resolution monochrome)
- A mouse
- A computer power supply (large plastic box)
- A disk-drive power supply (smaller plastic box)
- A disk-drive cable
- A video cable
- A video-display AC power cable.

While your system may include additional components, all systems include this basic equipment. This chapter identifies each component and connector

FIGURE 1-1. Equipment included with the Atari 520-ST

provided by Atari and introduces the function of each.

Place the 520-ST on a flat surface, such as the top of a table. Make sure that you have room to put the monitor near the computer; the best place for it is directly behind the computer.

REAR AND SIDE PANELS

All of the switches, connectors, and interfaces are located at the sides and the back of the 520-ST. These components are labeled in Figure 1-2. It is important that you learn the function and location of each component as you hook up the computer to avoid damaging it by using connections incorrectly.

The ON/OFF Power Switch

Make sure the 520-ST is turned off before you begin. The ON/OFF power switch is at the rear of the computer. It is a two-position "rocker" switch.

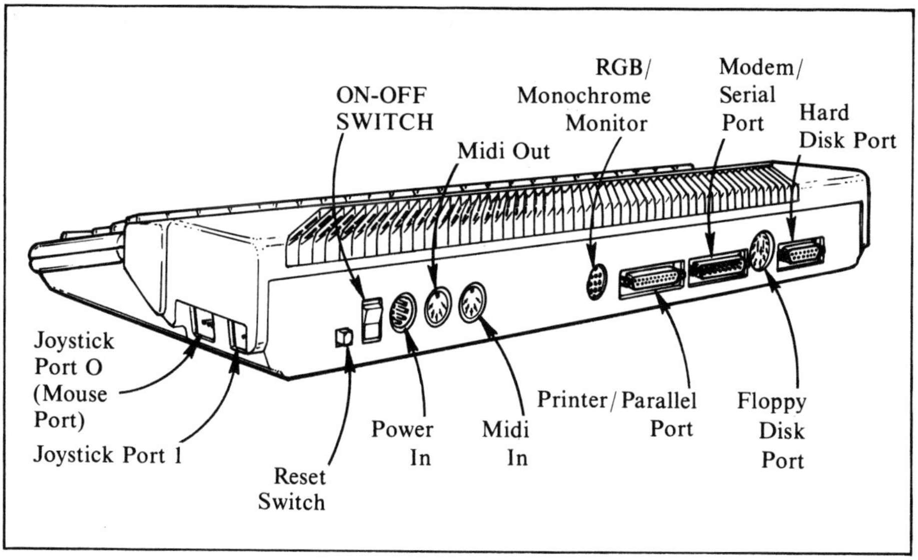

FIGURE 1-2. Rear and side view of the Atari 520-ST

Later, when you first turn on the ST, it will initialize itself. It will check out its internal systems and memory and load from the disk the information that it needs to operate.

When you turn the power off, all programs and data in memory that were not stored onto the diskette will be lost.

Power Connector

The computer power supply has two cables attached to it. One plugs into any standard 110-volt AC outlet, and the other plugs directly into the power connector next to the ON/OFF power switch on the rear of the ST.

Reset Button

Pressing the Reset button, which is next to the power switch, has the same effect as turning the power off and then on again—it restarts the system. This is sometimes called a *warm start* or *warm boot*.

Game/Mouse Ports

There are two 9-pin game connectors on the right side of the ST; they are labeled 0 and 1. These connectors are used for the various game controllers available for the ST, such as the mouse, joysticks, paddle controllers, and track balls. In normal operation, the mouse must be connected to game port 0.

Midi Ports

The Midi ports are used to communicate with special electronic musical instruments and devices. With the proper programming, your ST can be used to control these devices.

Monitor Port

The ST can use two different video displays: an RGB color monitor, or a high-resolution monochrome (black-and-white) monitor. If you install a monochrome monitor, the ST will automatically detect it and set the display for the highest resolution (640×400 dots). If you connect an RGB monitor, the ST will give you the option of using either medium resolution (640×200 dots) or low resolution (320×200 dots).

The 520-ST displays characters in one of two modes: 8×8 or 8×16, as shown in Figure 1-3. The 8×8 mode is used in low-resolution mode only (320×200 dots). The other two screen modes (medium and high resolution) use the 8×16 character sets.

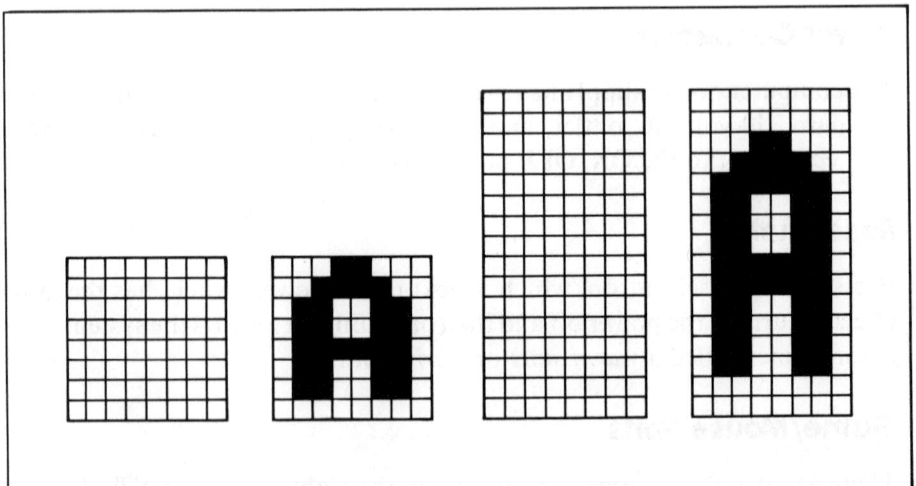

FIGURE 1-3. The 8×8 and 8×16 character displays

NOTE: For a complete listing of the 256 Atari characters, see Appendix A at the end of this book.

Printer/Parallel Port

The printer port has been designed to work with standard Atari ST parallel printers or any Epson or Epson-type parallel printer. The printer port supports standard Centronics-type parallel data signals; advanced users may program this port for special applications.

Modem/Serial Port

The modem port is a standard RS232C serial port that can be used with such serial devices as modems and serial printers. (Instructions for configuring this and other ports are provided later in this chapter.)

Floppy Disk Interface

You must use at least one floppy disk drive to operate your 520-ST. The drive that comes with the ST is capable of storing almost half a million bytes of information on a single disk. The ST can operate two floppy disk drives.

Hard Disk Interface

The hard disk interface is designed to connect only to an Atari hard disk drive. Although hard disk drives are more expensive than floppy drives, they are many times faster and hold much more information.

Cartridge/Expansion Port

The cartridge port is typically used to insert programs or games into the ST. This port can also be used as an expansion port for the ST, allowing access to the internal data and address lines.

SETTING UP THE SYSTEM

In this section you will connect the various parts of the ST together, using the cables provided.

WARNING: Do not yet turn on any of these devices or the computer. Wait until all of the components are connected properly and you have checked all of the connections.

Video Display

The 520-ST works with either the Atari SM124 monochrome monitor (black-and-white) or the Atari SC1224 monitor (RGB analog color). These both have the same connectors, and the ST automatically determines which monitor is connected. Follow these steps to connect your monitor:

1. Connect the video-display cable to the rear of the video display and to the connector labeled "Monitor" at the rear of the ST, as shown in Figure 1-4.
2. Connect the female end of the video-display AC cable to the rear of the video display (see Figure 1-5), and plug the male end into a standard 110-volt AC wall outlet.

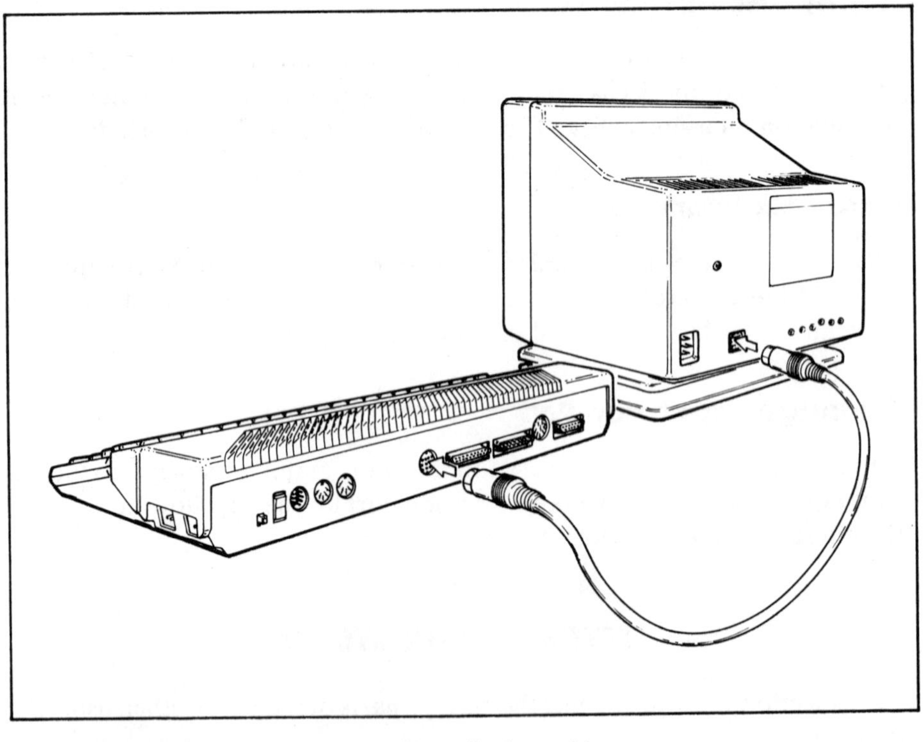

FIGURE 1-4. Connecting the video-display cable

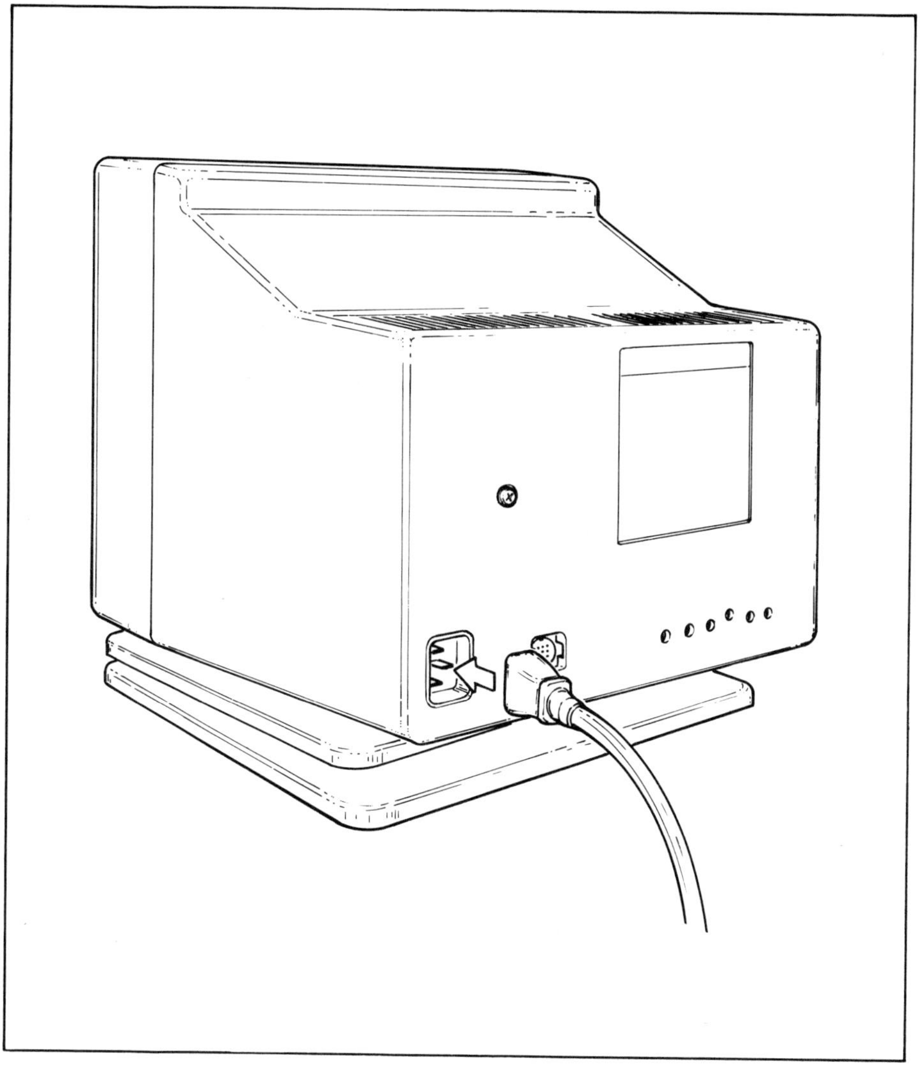

FIGURE 1-5. The monitor power cable

Disk Drives

There are two kinds of disk drives available for the ST. One is a 500K disk drive (like the one that came with the system), and the other is a 1M (one million byte) drive. If you have only one drive, read these directions and skip

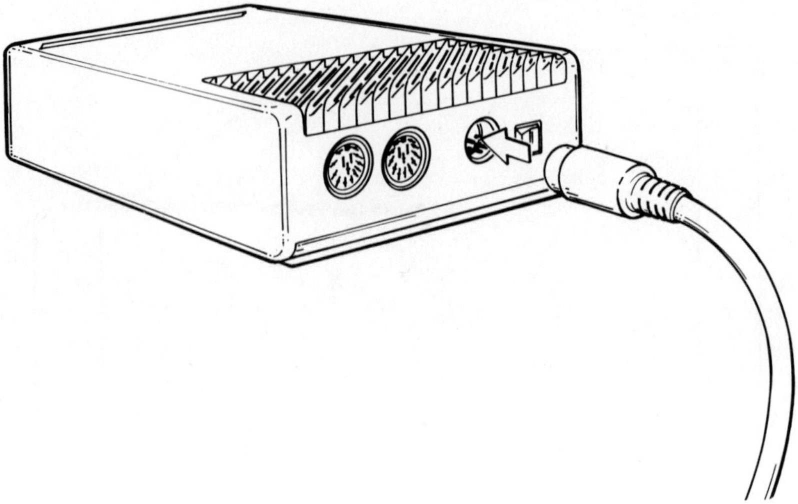

FIGURE 1-6. Connecting power to the disk drives

the section on installing a second disk drive.

1. The disk-drive power supply has two cables attached to it. One plugs into a standard 110-volt AC outlet. The other plugs directly into the power connector at the rear of the disk drive (the small, round connector next to the ON/OFF switch, as shown in Figure 1-6).
2. The disk-drive data cable has identical large, round connectors at both ends. Plug one end into the connector labeled "Floppy Disk" at the rear of the ST, as shown in Figure 1-7.
3. Plug the other end of the disk-drive data cable into the connector labeled "IN" at the rear of the disk drive (see Figure 1-8).

INSTALLING A SECOND DISK DRIVE

Here are the steps for installing a second disk drive:

1. The second disk drive uses a separate power supply that is exactly like the first one and has two cables attached to it. One plugs into any

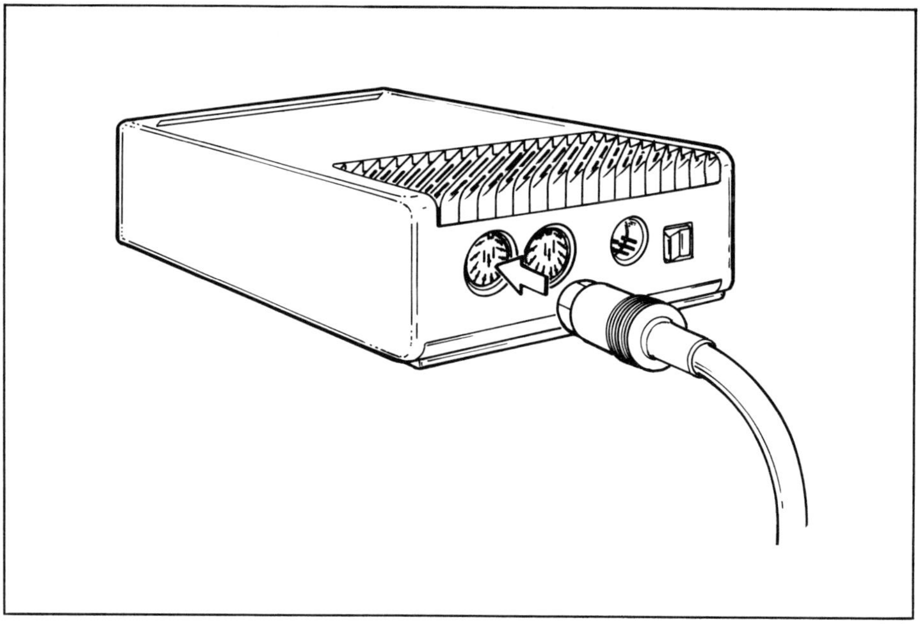

FIGURE 1-7. Drive A data-cable connection

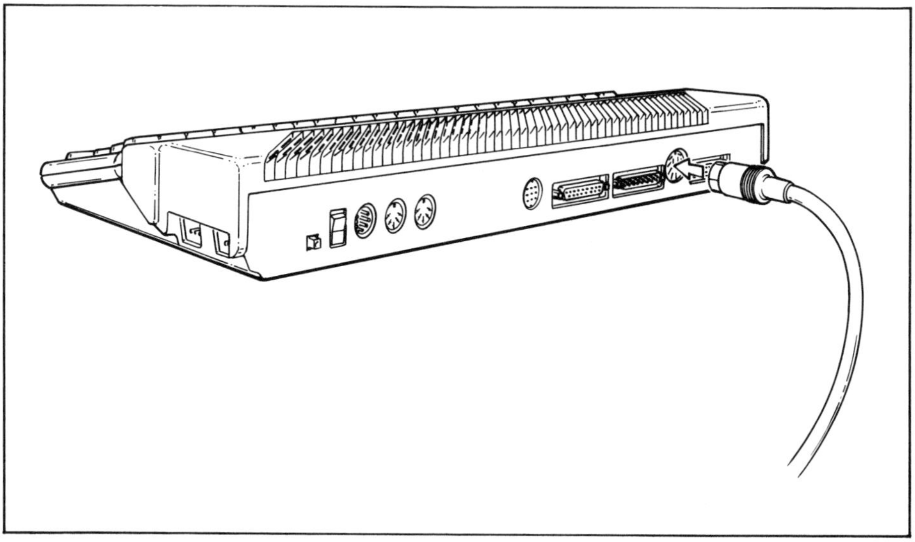

FIGURE 1-8. Connecting the disk-drive data cable to the ST

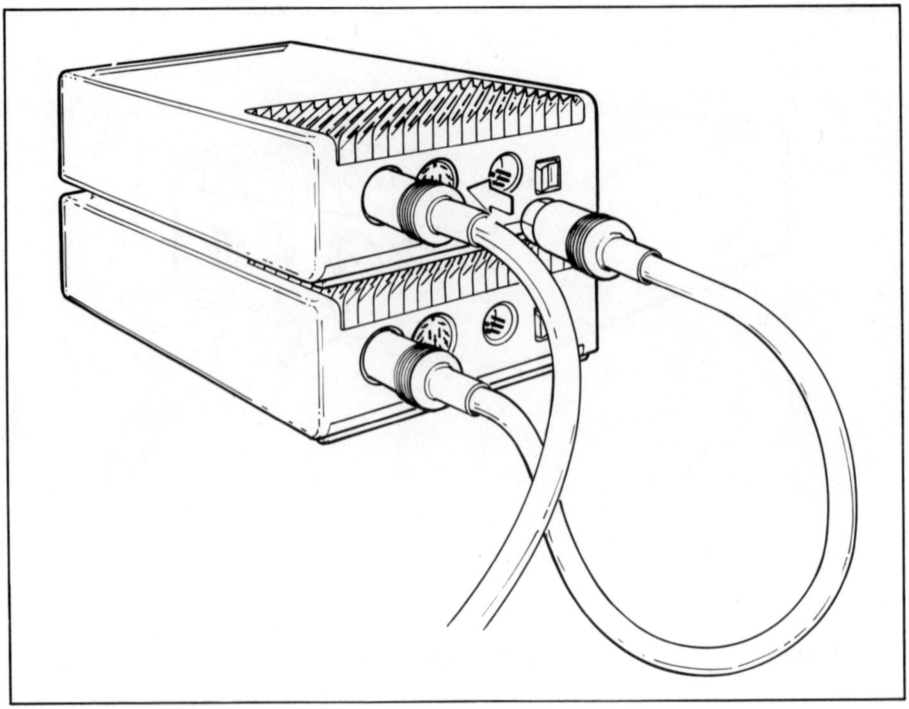

FIGURE 1-9. Daisy-chaining the disk drives

standard 110-volt AC outlet. The other plugs directly into the power connector at the rear of the second disk drive (the small, round connector directly beside the ON/OFF switch).

2. The second disk-drive data cable also has identical large, round connectors at both ends. Plug one end into the first "Floppy Disk" connector labeled "OUT" at the rear of the ST.

3. Plug the other end of the second disk-drive data cable into the connector at the rear of the second disk drive labeled "IN" (see Figure 1-9). This is known as *daisy-chaining* the drives.

Attaching the Mouse

The mouse has a single wire attached to it. Plug its connector into game port 0, as shown in Figure 1-10. When you use the mouse, hold it so that its cable is located away from you, as shown here:

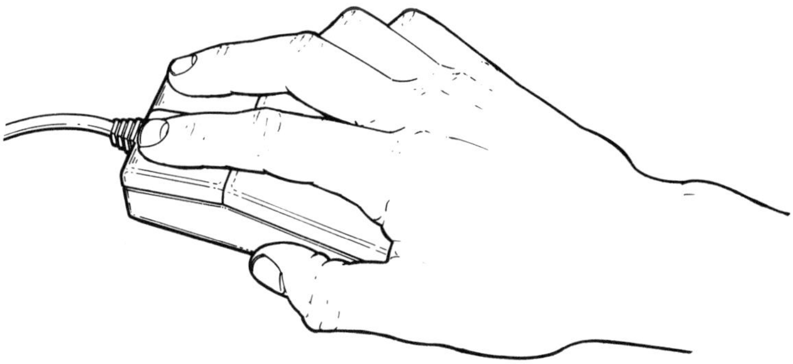

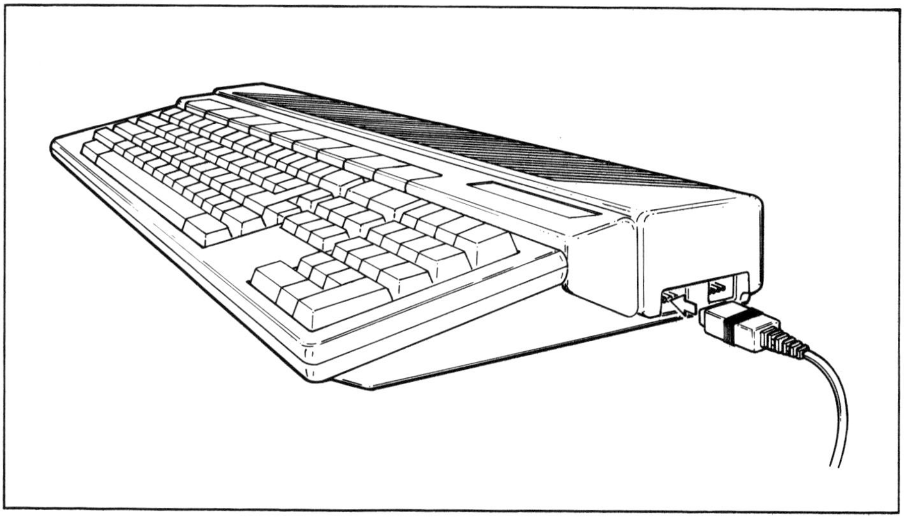

FIGURE 1-10. Connecting the mouse

The Computer Power Supply

The computer power supply is a large black plastic box that has two cables attached to it. One plugs into a standard 110-volt AC outlet. The other plugs directly into the power connector at the rear of the computer (the small, round connector directly beside the ON/OFF switch), as shown in Figure 1-11.

Powering Up

Before you turn on the power, there is one more thing that you need to do: insert the TOS disk into the first disk drive (also called drive A). To insert the disk in the disk drive, hold it so that the metal shutter is away from you (toward the disk drive) and the larger part of the disk label is facing up, as shown in Figure 1-12.

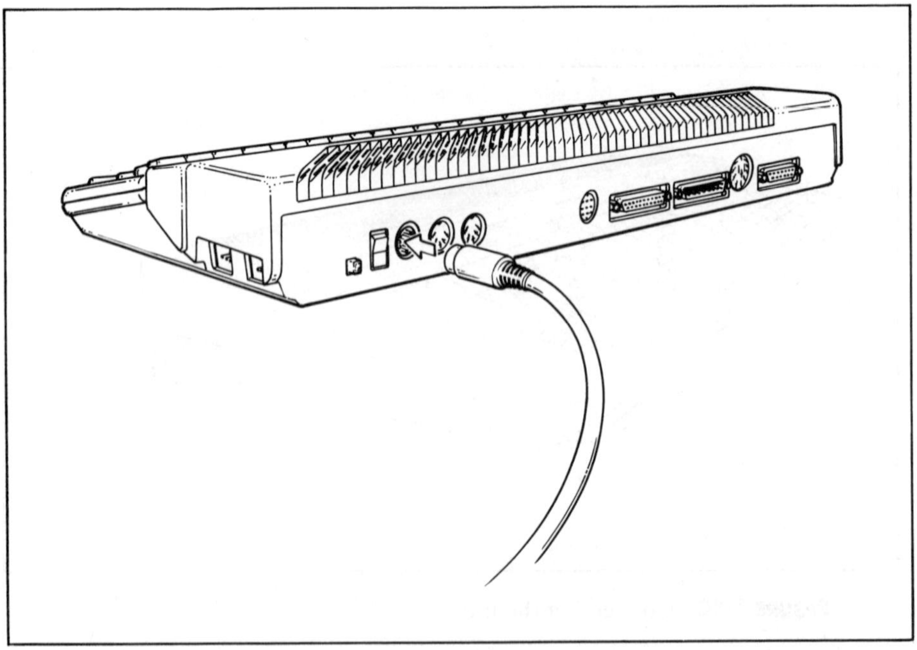

FIGURE 1-11. Attaching the computer power supply

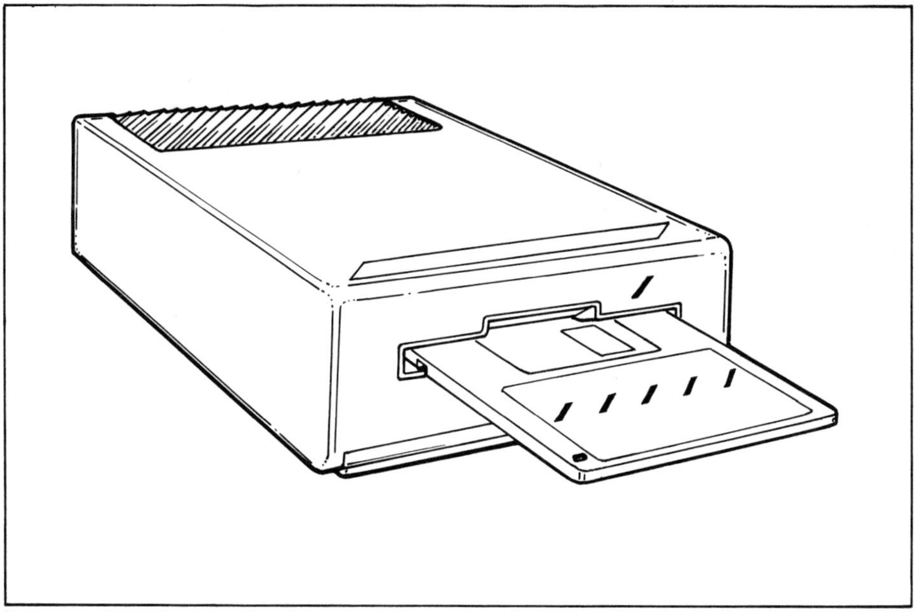

FIGURE 1-12. Inserting a floppy disk

Push the disk all the way into the disk drive until you hear a click and the disk "drops" into position.

WARNING: If the disk does not push in smoothly and easily, *do not force it*—you might damage it. Pull it out and try again.

Finally, double-check all of the connections you have just made. It is very important that every component be connected correctly. After you are satisfied that all of the connections are correct, turn on the power switches in the following order:

1. Turn on the monitor.
2. Turn on the disk drive(s).
3. Turn on the computer.

Once you have turned the power on, the 520-ST will display the screen at the top of the next page on a color display.

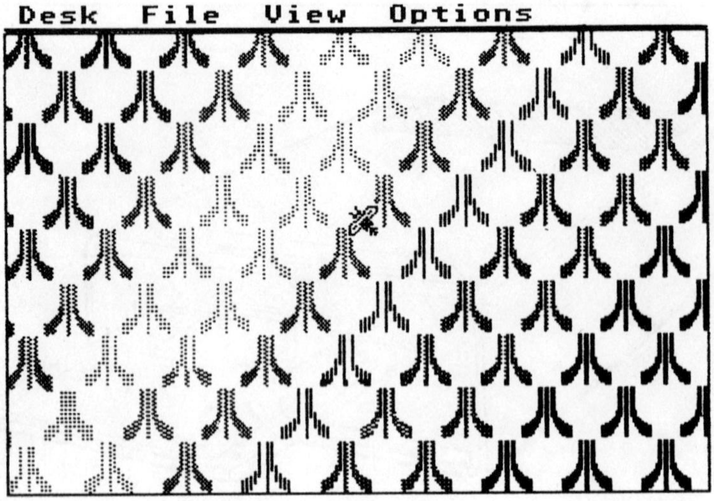

If you have a monochrome display, the ST will produce this display:

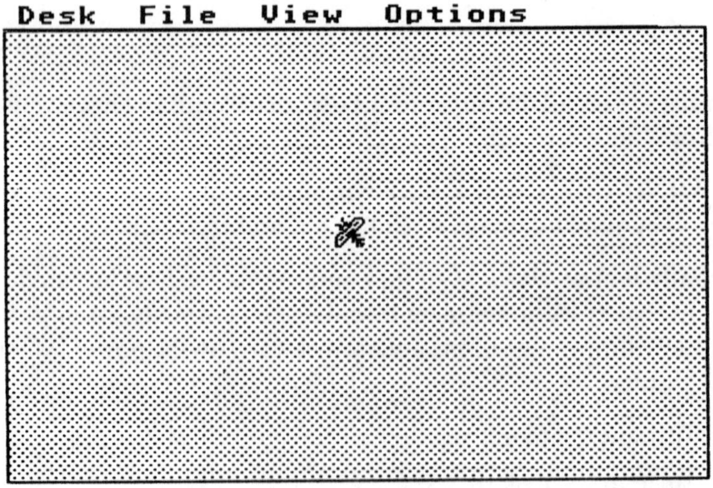

After a few moments, the ST will produce the following desktop:

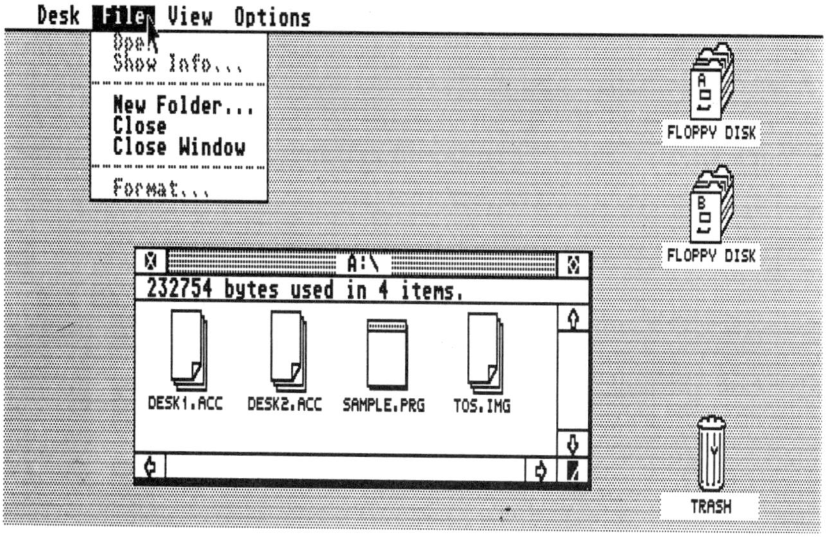

If, instead of the desktop, you see a display like this:

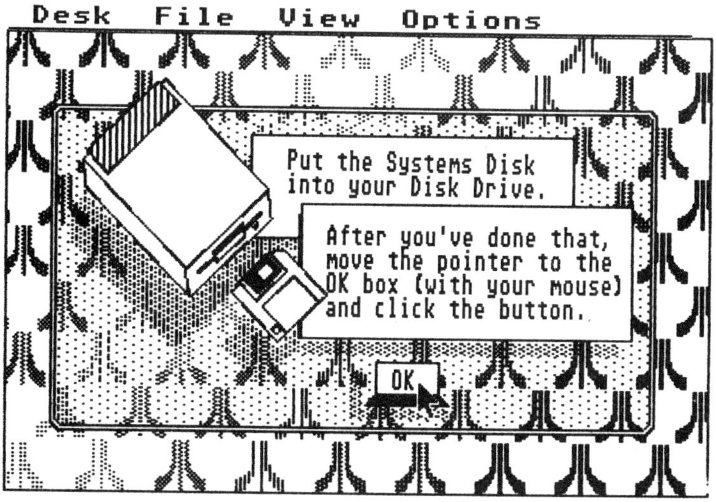

then you have a problem with the disk drive. Double-check the disk-drive connections and the disk itself. Is the disk not in straight? Is one of the cables not in all the way?

Remember, the disk must be in drive A. If you have two drives, drive A is the one that has two cables attached to the computer. Drive B has only one cable connected to the computer; the other is attached to drive A, as shown below.

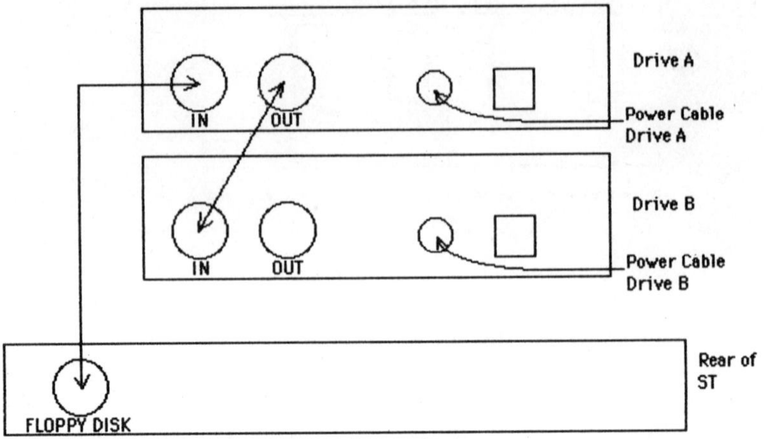

Also make sure that the disk you have inserted is labeled TOS. Once you have corrected any incorrect connections or replaced the disk, press the RETURN key on the keyboard, and the ST will try to start again.

If, after you have checked all of your connections thoroughly and have confirmed that you are using the right disk, you still do not get the desktop display, contact your Atari dealer.

THE MOUSE

Most computers offer only one method of entering information directly into the computer: the keyboard. While the ST has an extensive keyboard, it also provides you with another method of communication: the mouse. Operating the mouse is a simple process, but it does take a little practice. Here are a few tips that will help.

- Place the mouse on a flat surface that is at least 12×12 inches. While this is not essential, you will be less likely to run off the edge of your table with the mouse as you operate it.

- Always position the mouse with its cable pointing away from you.

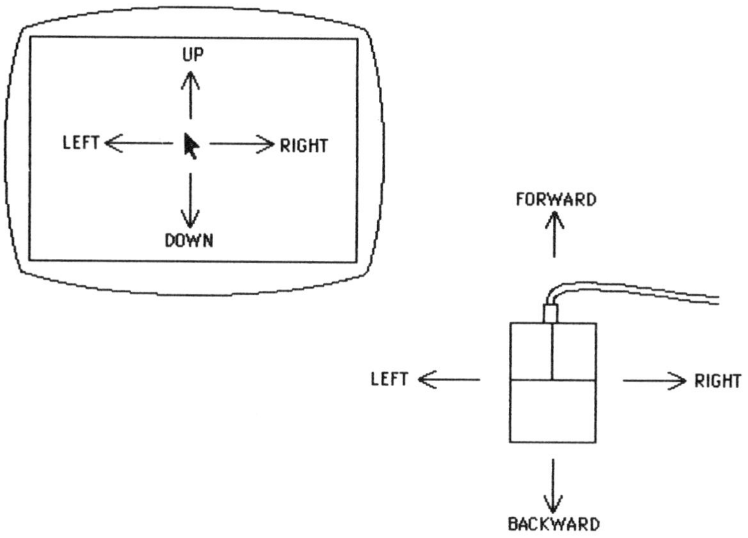

- The mouse has two buttons, which are called the left button and the right button. For all of the operations in this book, you'll use the left button unless otherwise specified.

Moving the Mouse

In general, the mouse is used to position a small arrow (called the *pointer*) on the screen. The mouse translates movement on your table to movement on the screen. For example, if you move the mouse away from you on the table, the pointer on the screen will move up. If you move the mouse left, the pointer will move left. It is important, however, that you keep the mouse pointing directly away from you. If you do not, it is possible to get movement on the screen that may appear to be erratic.

To get an idea of how this may happen, turn the mouse slightly to the right and then move it directly away from you, as shown in the following illustration.

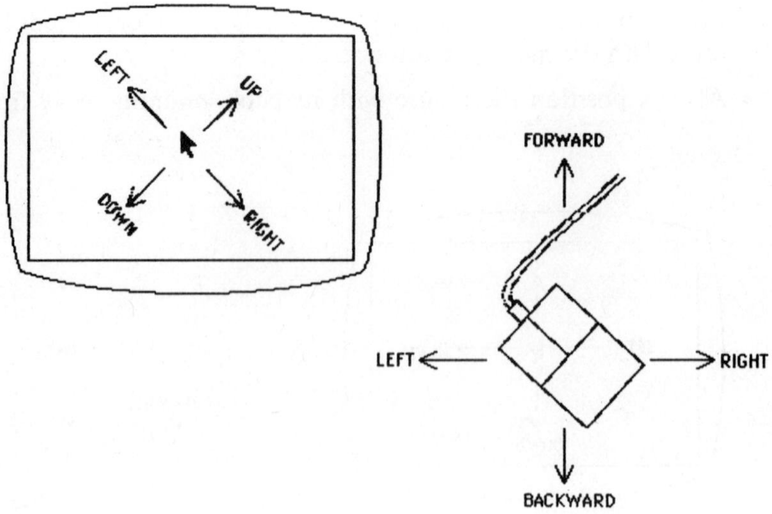

Notice how the pointer moves diagonally instead of straight up. If you feel more comfortable holding the mouse at a slight angle, you will need to compensate for that angle in your movements.

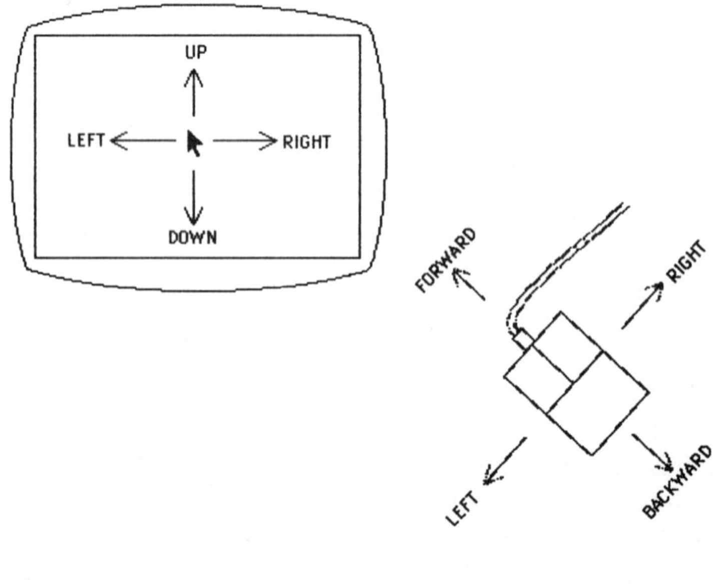

POINTING

Before you begin this section, take a few moments to practice moving the mouse and watching the result on the screen. Move it up and down, left and right. Move it in circles. When you feel comfortable with the mouse, read on. In this section, you will start using the mouse for practical applications.

SELECTING OBJECTS: THE TIP OF THE ARROW

On the desktop, the main purpose of the pointer is to select objects and move them around. This will be covered in considerable detail in the next chapter, but for the moment, you should take a quick look at how this works.

Although the mouse pointer can take many forms (that of a bumble bee, for example), most of the time it will be an arrow. To select something on the screen, you will need to point at it with the pointer. For example, try pointing at the small picture of a filing drawer in the upper-left corner of the screen. Small pictures on the desktop like the drawer and the trash can are called *icons.*

When you point at the drawer, you must be sure that the tip of the arrow is inside the icon. The tip of the arrow is called the *hot spot.* To select the icon, make sure the hot spot is inside the icon and press the left mouse button (remember that you will almost always use the left mouse button).

When you select an icon, that icon will turn black. To deselect an icon, point the arrow anywhere else on the desktop and press the mouse button again. Practice pointing and selecting the various objects on the desktop.

THE KEYBOARD

Before you begin learning about the keyboard, you should know that some of the examples shown in this section make use of the LOGO programming language. Although LOGO has not yet been presented in this book, you may wish to try the examples as you read them. To try the examples if you have only one disk drive, remove the TOS disk from the disk drive by pressing the

Eject button on the front of the disk drive. If you have two disk drives, leave the TOS disk in drive A and simply put the LOGO language disk in drive B.

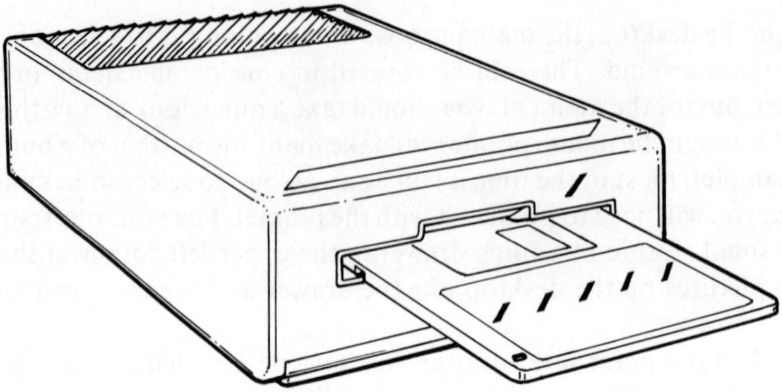

Insert the LOGO disk in the disk drive and select the file-drawer icon labeled "B" (point to the icon and press the mouse button). Then point to the menu (at the top of the desktop) labeled "File". The File menu will drop down and reveal the following:

Move the pointer down until the word "Open" is highlighted, and then click the mouse button. After a few moments, the LOGO Dialog window and the Graphics Display window will appear. Type the word **EDIT** and press RETURN. Then point with the pointer to the small symbol in the upper-right corner of the Edit window and click the mouse button.

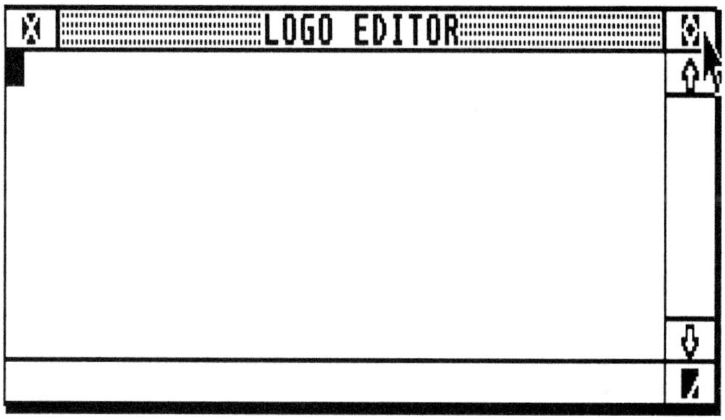

A Tour of the Keyboard

In almost every application, the keyboard is used to communicate with the 520-ST. The keys are arranged much like those on a standard typewriter; however, there are many more keys on the ST than on any standard typewriter. In addition, unlike typewriter keys, each of the ST's keys can be used to access as many as three or four different symbols or functions.

The keys on the ST may be classified as follows:

- Alphabetic keys
- Numeric keys
- Function keys
- Cursor/pointer control keys.

ALPHABETIC KEYS

The alphabetic keys include the 26 letters of the alphabet in both upper- and lowercase. When the ST is powered up, the letters are displayed in lowercase on the desktop. To print uppercase letters, press either of the two SHIFT keys. If you are typing quite a few uppercase letters at one time, you may choose to press the CAPS LOCK key.

NOTE: Some programs like LOGO require that all commands be entered in uppercase. As such, LOGO automatically configures the keyboard so it will print only uppercase letters. You may switch to upper- or lowercase simply by pressing the CAPS LOCK key.

NUMERIC KEYS

Numeric keys are used to enter the digits 0 through 9. The ST has two sets of numeric keys; one is along the top of the typewriter keys, and the other is in the numeric keypad. In most applications these keys operate identically, but they can be programmed to have different values or functions.

FUNCTION KEYS

Any key that "does something" rather than "prints something" is a function key. For instance, CAPS LOCK doesn't print anything, but it causes all subsequent characters to be displayed in uppercase on the screen. The function keys—SHIFT, CAPS LOCK, RETURN, and the cursor control keys—are shown in Figure 1-13.

The SHIFT key is used in conjunction with any key on the keyboard to access the key's "shifted" character or function. For example, shifted lowercase letters become uppercase letters, while a shifted number 7 becomes an ampersand (&).

There are two identical SHIFT keys on the ST keyboard. One is at the lower-left corner of the keyboard above the ALTERNATE key, while the other is to the right of the space bar, just above the CAPS LOCK key.

The RETURN key is similar to the carriage return on a typewriter. It causes the *cursor* (the small black square that indicates where the next character will appear) to return to the left-hand margin of the next line.

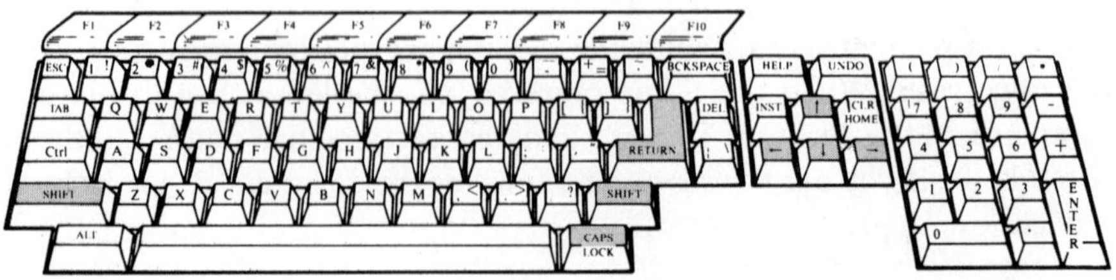

FIGURE 1-13. Function keys

The RETURN key is also used to enter instructions in LOGO. After keying in a line of your procedure or program, you press RETURN to enter that line into memory.

Pressing RETURN while the cursor is at the bottom of the window will cause all of the text in that window to scroll up, moving the cursor to the beginning of the new, blank line generated by the scroll.

CURSOR/POINTER KEYS

The remaining keys—CLR/HOME, ALTERNATE, CONTROL, INSERT, HELP, UNDO, and SHIFT—all move the cursor in some way. They are highlighted in Figure 1-14.

In LOGO, the CLR/HOME key moves the cursor back to the upper-left corner of the Edit window. The four arrow keys (also called cursor control keys) move the cursor up, down, left, and right within the text area of the window. If you press and hold the down-arrow key, the cursor will continue moving down until it reaches the bottom of the text you entered. You cannot move the cursor outside of the text area with the cursor control keys. The up-, left-, and right-arrow keys work in exactly the same way as the down-arrow key, moving the cursor as indicated.

If you are at the end of a line, the INSERT key inserts a new blank line below the current line. If you are in the middle of a line, the INSERT key moves the remainder of the current line down to the beginning of the next line.

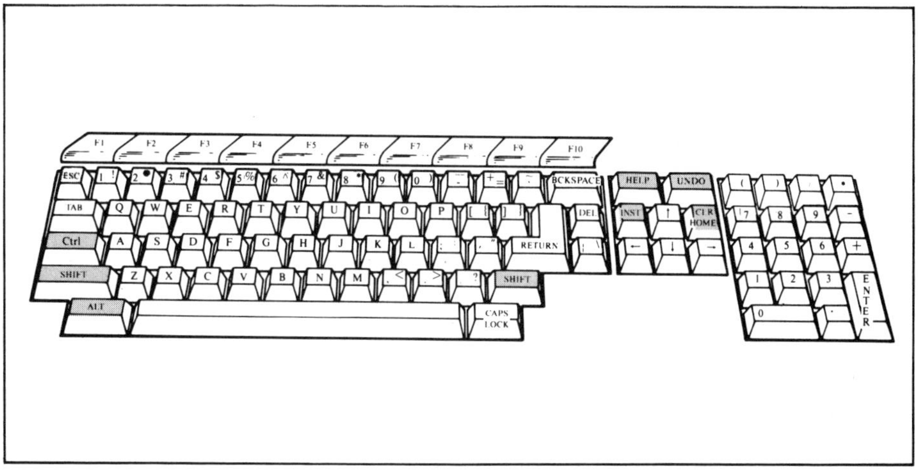

FIGURE 1-14. Cursor/pointer control keys

MOUSE-POINTER CONTROL

In addition to moving the cursor in the window, the arrow keys can also move the mouse pointer. To move the mouse pointer, hold down the ALTERNATE key (immediately to the left of the space bar) and press any one of the arrow keys. The mouse pointer will start moving in one-character increments in the direction you select.

If you hold down both the ALTERNATE and the SHIFT keys and then press one of the arrow keys, the mouse pointer will move in the selected direction in one-dot increments.

You can produce left and right button-presses by holding the ALTERNATE key and pressing the INSERT key (for the left mouse button) or the CLR/HOME key (for the right button).

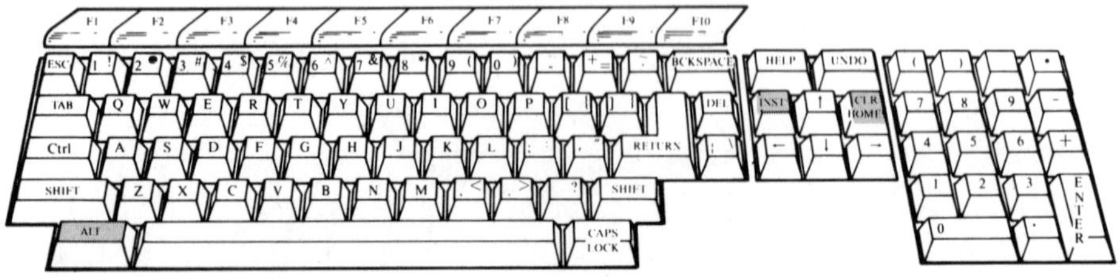

By using these key combinations, you can keep your hands on the keyboard at all times. This can make word processing and similar programs simpler to use, since you won't have to stop in the middle of an operation to grab the mouse.

Programmable Function Keys

In addition to the keys just described, the ST has ten programmable, four-function keys, labeled F1 through F10. Each can be used alone or with the SHIFT key, the CONTROL key, or the ALTERNATE key. The functions of these keys are specified by the user or by the program that you are currently running.

CHAPTER

The Desktop 2

In Chapter 1 you looked at the basic components of the Atari 520 ST. These are the computer, the disk drives, a video display, and the mouse. You also learned to connect these together to make a complete, working system. In this chapter you'll take a look at the way the ST operates and how you can communicate with it.

SCREENS AND WINDOWS

Like most computers, the ST presents most of its information to you through a video display. Unlike most computers, however, the ST's display can be divided up into several separate viewing and operating areas called *windows*. All of the ST's programs run in one or more of these windows.

Figure 2-1 shows a picture of a window that contains text. As you can see, some of the words have been cut off at the sides, and some lines are hidden by the top and the bottom of the window. Obviously, you should be able to see

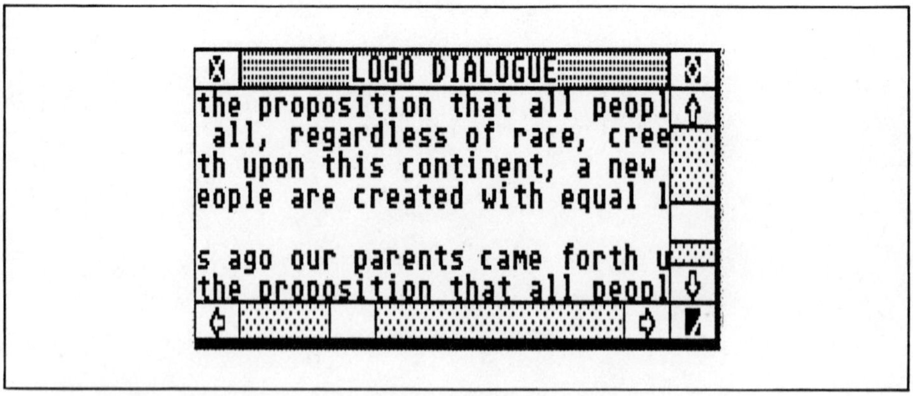
LOGO DIALOGUE
the proposition that all peopl
all, regardless of race, cree
th upon this continent, a new
eople are created with equal l
s ago our parents came forth u
the proposition that all peopl

FIGURE 2-1. A typical ST window

more of this text. The window is like a viewport through which you can see some or all of a screen area.

You can see more or less of the text by making the window larger or smaller with the window controls. Here, the window is larger:

LOGO DIALOGUE
al years ago our parents came forth u
ted to the proposition that all peopl
ice for all, regardless of race, cree
me forth upon this continent, a new
t all people are created with equal l
al years ago our parents came forth u
ted to the proposition that all peopl
ice for all, regardless of race, cree

You can *scroll* (move) the contents of the window up, down, left, or right:

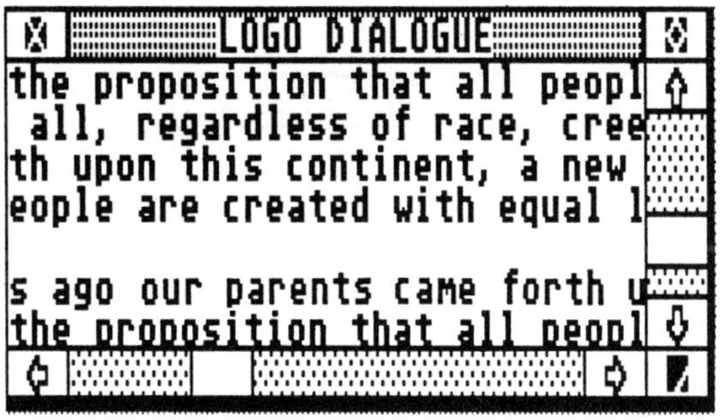

You can also *close* the window to put it away:

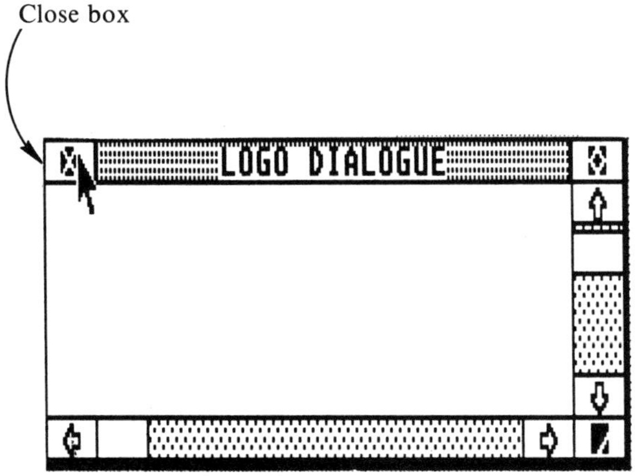

The window controls are located at the corners and sides of the window. They are

- Scroll up arrow
- Scroll down arrow
- Scroll right arrow
- Scroll left arrow
- Horizontal scroll bar
- Vertical scroll bar

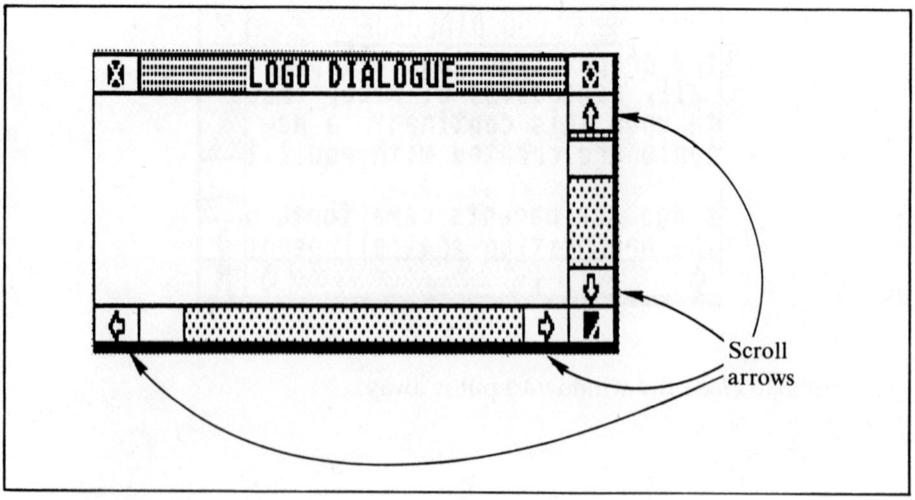

FIGURE 2-2. The scroll arrows

- Size box
- Full box
- Close box
- Move/title bar.

Scrolling Windows

If you look closely at Figure 2-2, you will see that there are four small, outlined arrows at the right side and the bottom of the window. These are the *scroll arrows.* They move the window left, right, up, or down across the document. To get an idea of how they work, point at the up arrow with the mouse pointer and click the left mouse button once.

This moved the contents of the window down to reveal a new line above the previous text.

Remember: the window is a viewport that moves around on top of the document, so when you scroll the window up, the document appears to move down inside the window.

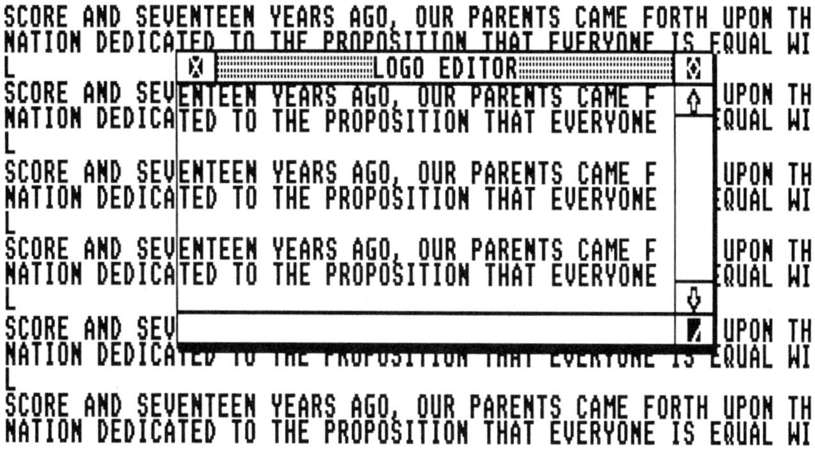

Similarily, when you scroll the window right (by clicking the right scroll arrow), the text will actually move to the left.

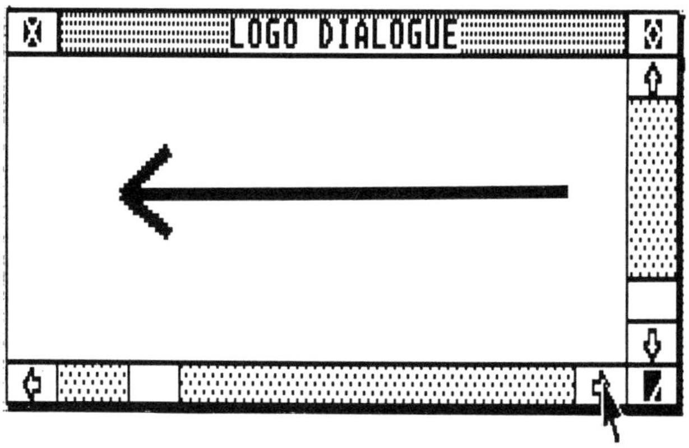

Size Box

The Size box (in the lower-right corner of the window) allows you to enlarge or reduce the size of the window. To resize a window, point at the Size box with the mouse pointer: then press and hold down the left mouse button until a faint rectangle appears inside the outline of the window.

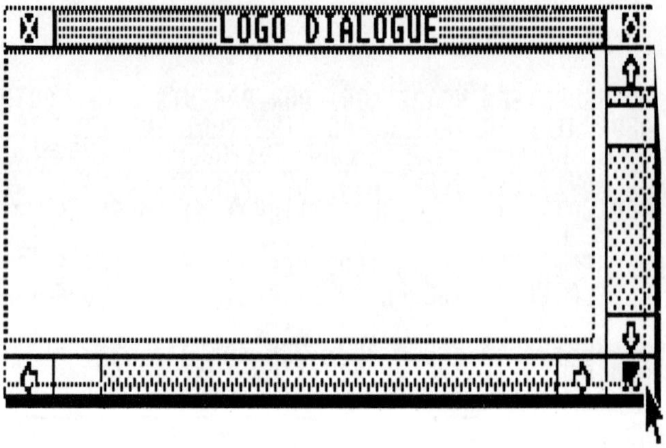

Continue holding down the mouse button, and move the mouse up, down, left, or right until the outline window is the size and shape you want. Then release the mouse button.

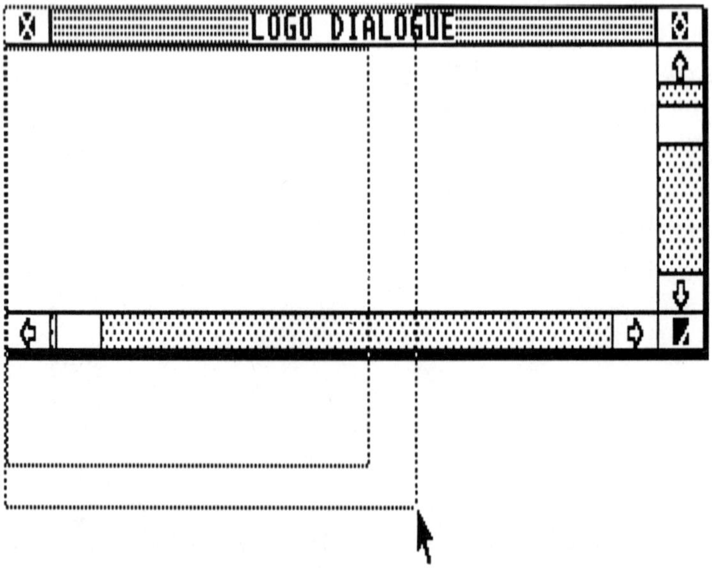

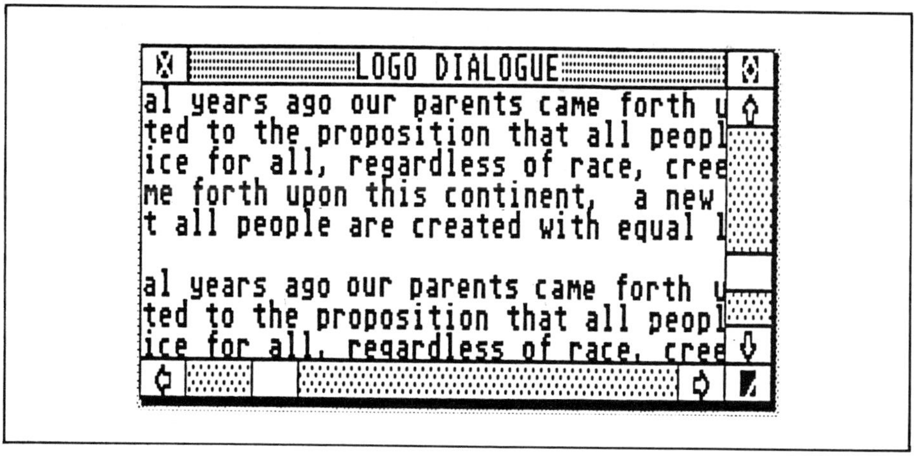
LOGO DIALOGUE
al years ago our parents came forth u
ted to the proposition that all peopl
ice for all, regardless of race, cree
me forth upon this continent, a new
t all people are created with equal l
al years ago our parents came forth u
ted to the proposition that all peopl
ice for all, regardless of race, cree

FIGURE 2-3. Adjusting the window size

Scroll Bars and Boxes

The scroll bars serve two functions. First, they are indicators, showing how much of the document is visible. This is determined by the size of the Scroll box. In Figure 2-3, for example, the horizontal Scroll box is half as wide as the horizontal scroll bar. This means that half of the horizontal view of the document is currently visible in the window. If you make the window smaller, the Scroll box will become proportionally smaller.

If you expand the window until it shows the entire document, the Scroll box will grow to fill the entire scroll bar, indicating that there is nothing hidden beyond the edges of the window, except in Logo, where there is no indication.

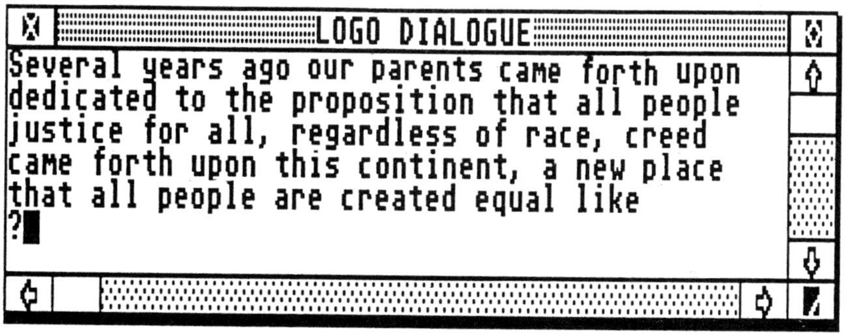
LOGO DIALOGUE
Several years ago our parents came forth upon
dedicated to the proposition that all people
justice for all, regardless of race, creed
came forth upon this continent, a new place
that all people are created equal like
?

In addition to functioning as indicators, Scroll boxes can also move the contents of the window. To scroll with the Scroll boxes, point the mouse pointer at the Scroll box and press and hold down the left mouse button. When a dotted outline appears in the box, you can drag it along the length of the scroll bar. When you release the button, the window contents will be moved the appropriate distance in the indicated direction.

For example, the Scroll box in Figure 2-4 is at the top of the vertical scroll bar. Although we could scroll down to the bottom of the document by repeatedly clicking the down arrow, it is quicker to simply drag the vertical Scroll box to the bottom of the vertical scroll bar.

The Full Box

Clicking the Full box, located at the upper righthand corner of the screen, instantly expands the window to make it fill the desktop.

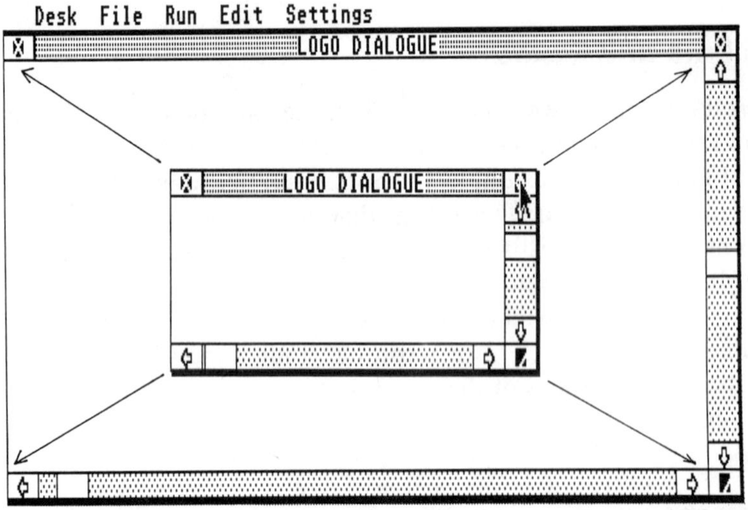

Clicking the Full box again (when the window is full-size) will shrink the window back to its previous size and location.

It is important to understand that Full is a *toggle* function. In other words, it will always make a smaller window fill the screen, but if you modify the full-size window in any way, it may not shrink down to its previous size properly.

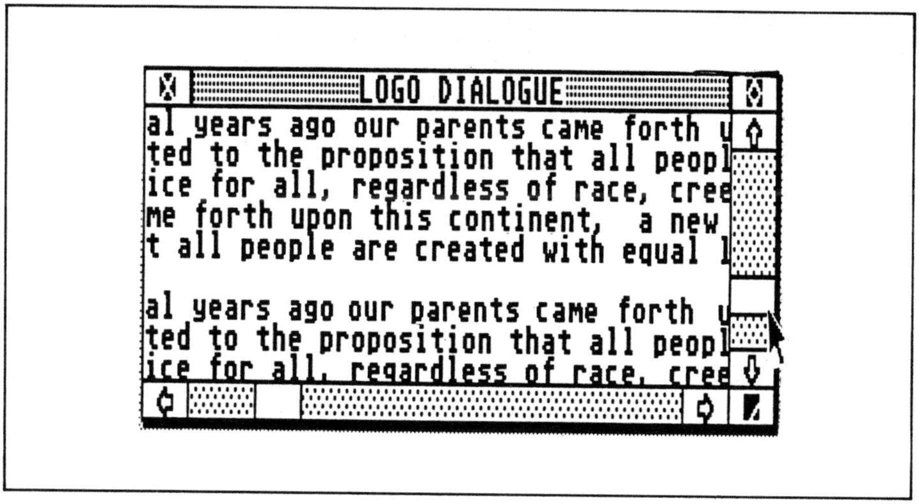
LOGO DIALOGUE
al years ago our parents came forth u
ted to the proposition that all peopl
ice for all, regardless of race, cree
me forth upon this continent, a new
t all people are created with equal l
al years ago our parents came forth u
ted to the proposition that all peopl
ice for all, regardless of race, cree

FIGURE 2-4. Dragging the Scroll box

For instance, a disk window is quite small, and you want to see all of its contents. Click the Full box, and the window expands to fill the screen:

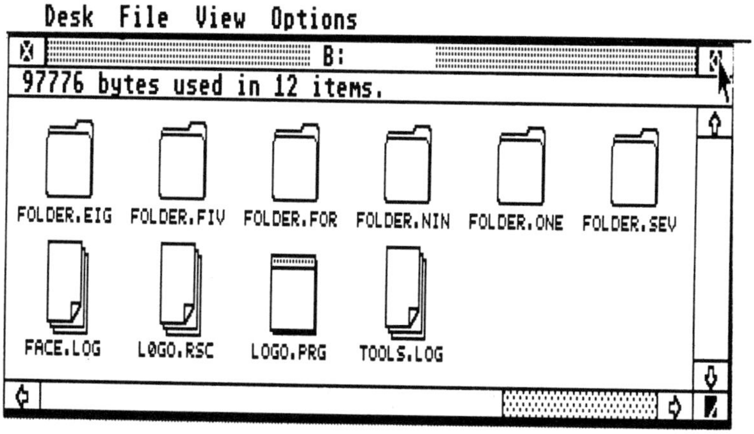
Desk File View Options
B:
97776 bytes used in 12 items.
FOLDER.EIG
FOLDER.FIV
FOLDER.FOR
FOLDER.NIN
FOLDER.ONE
FOLDER.SEV
FACE.LOG
LOGO.RSC
LOGO.PRG
TOOLS.LOG

You then decide that you only need to view the four icons at the left edge of the window. You use the Size box to show only those icons.

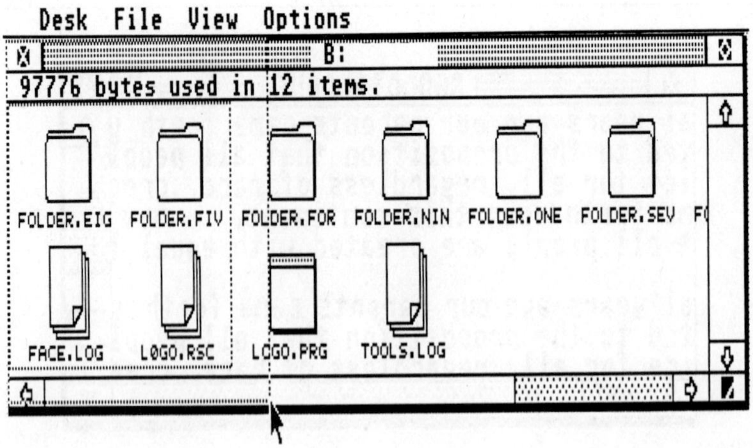

When you are done, you click the Full box to return the window to its original size; but instead, the box zooms up to fill the entire screen. This happens because the Full-box function only remembers the most recent size and position of the window since it was last clicked. Since you resized the window, the original data on size and position was replaced by the new size and position of the window with only four icons.

The Title Bar

In addition to making the windows larger or smaller on the desktop, you can also move them around. To move a window, first point the mouse pointer somewhere inside the window's title bar, the gray bar along the top of the window that contains the window's name. You should note that disk windows

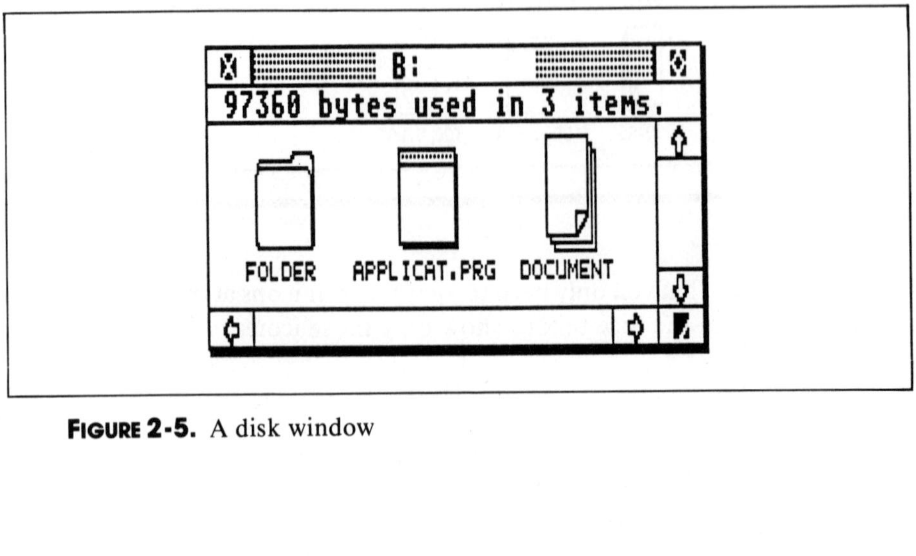

FIGURE 2-5. A disk window

are not named; they simply have the drive designation inside the title bar.

Next, press and hold down the left mouse button until a dotted line appears around the edge of the window. Then, while you continue to hold down the mouse button, drag the dotted outline to the new position you want, and release the button.

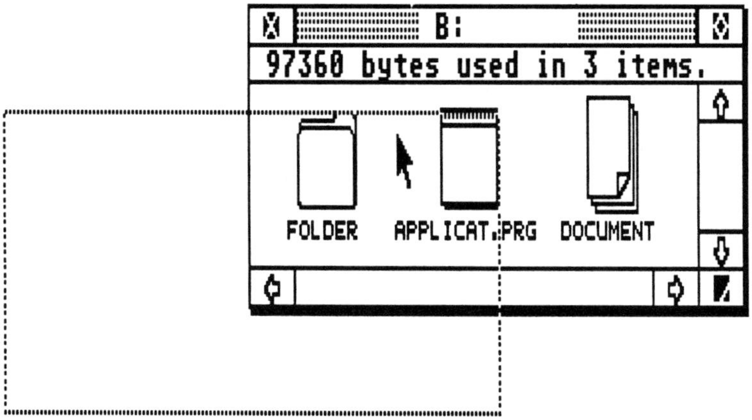

Close Box

The Close box "puts the window away." Since all windows are opened from icons, clicking on the Close box shrinks the window down and puts it back into its icon.

ICONS

Look at the window in Figure 2-5. It contains three small pictures that are labeled FOLDER, APPLICAT.PRG, and DOCUMENT. These small pictures are called *icons,* and they are pictorial representations of computer files. Every program or document that you create or use on the ST will have an associated icon.

As you can see, the ST uses many different kinds of icons. Application icons represent programs. For example, the LOGO program has an icon that looks like this:

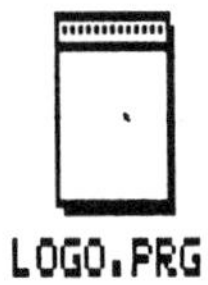

Programs always use this special icon. It provides you with an easy way of identifying the different kinds of items in a window.

Now look at the icon labeled DOCUMENT in Figure 2-5. This is not a program—it is a file that was created by a program. It contains only data. You cannot run a document file; it requires an associated program file. If you double-click a document icon that has no associated application, the ST will present this message box:

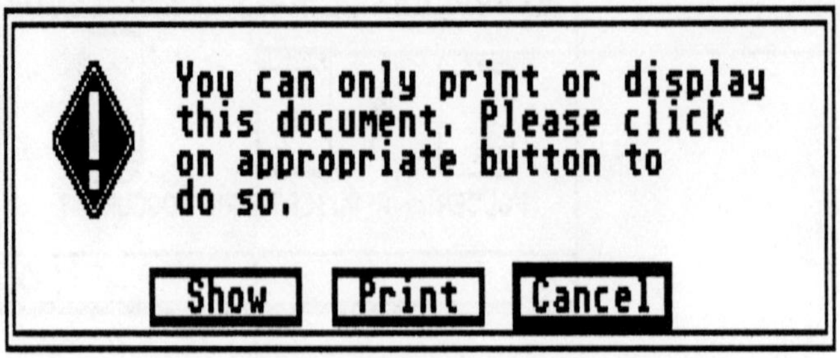
You can only print or display this document. Please click on appropriate button to do so.
Show
Print
Cancel

On the other hand, if you double-click on an icon and it does have an associated application (in other words, it was created by an existing application), it will load and run that application *and* the document.

NOTE: If the application that created the document is not present, you will get this message box:

This application can't find the folder or file you just tried to open.
OK

THE MENU BAR

In addition to the controls available to you in the windows and icons, the Atari ST provides a number of options and commands in the form of menus. These allow you to perform many of the functions that you will need to maintain your files and to customize your system.

Selecting Menus

There are four words printed at the top of the ST's desktop. They are Desk, File, View, and Options. These are the names of the four *desktop menus.* Pointing at any of these with the mouse button will highlight the menu name and reveal its options. For instance, the File menu looks like this:

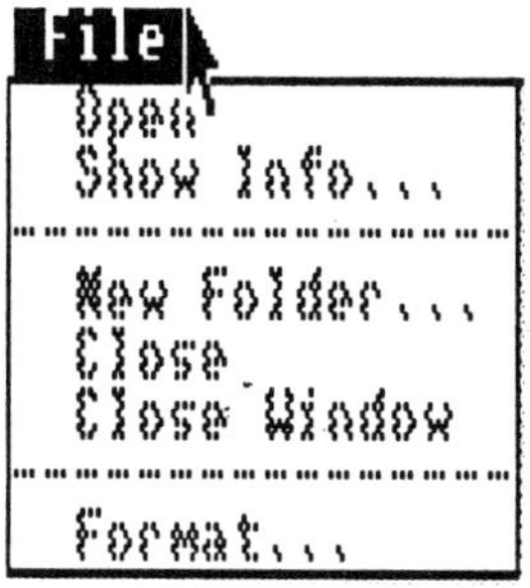

If you miss the menu you want and accidentally select another menu, simply move the pointer left or right. As you pass over the different menu headings, they will be highlighted and present their various options.

The Desk Menu

The leftmost menu choice is Desk. Selecting the Desk menu will reveal the following options:

To select the options in the menu, move the pointer downward along the menu. As you do this, the various items will be highlighted one at a time. When the item you want is highlighted, click the left mouse button.

DESKTOP INFO...

When you select the item labeled "Desktop Info...", the ST will display a large message box in the center of the desktop, showing current information about the ATARI ST's operating system. To remove the message box, click in the OK box.

VT52 EMULATOR

When the ST is running the VT52 emulator, it operates like a standard computer terminal, transmitting and receiving data through the modem port at the rear of the computer. In this mode the ST can operate any standard modem, allowing you to access computer networks and on-line services through your telephone line.

When you run the emulator, the desktop will disappear and the terminal screen will replace it. When this screen appears, you have three options.

The first option is to start typing. Any text or commands you type will be transmitted to the device you connect to the modem port. If the device is a modem, you will be able, simply by typing, to send data through the telephone lines to any other computer that is similarly connected. Whatever you type on the computer will appear on the other computer's display, and any data that is sent to you through the modem will be displayed on your screen as it is sent.

A second option when the terminal screen appears is to press the HELP key on the keyboard to "set up" (configure the terminal). This lets you change the settings on the RS232 serial port. When you press the HELP key, the ST will present a window with the information that enables you to to modify the following communication parameters.

- *Baud Rate:* This means the speed at which data is transmitted and received. The options are 9600, 4800, 1200, and 300 baud (bits per second). You should set these to match the speed that is specified by the device you connect to the port.

- *Parity:* This is a process that most serial devices use to check the data that they send and receive. All digital transmissions are combinations of binary numbers. A system that uses the parity of these numbers sets a separate bit in the data stream that will make all of the binary numbers either odd or even. It doesn't matter which method is used, as long as both the sender and receiver use the same parity. Your choices are Odd, Even, or None (if one or the other computer does not use the parity system).

- *Duplex:* When you type a character on the keyboard, your computer will ordinarily display that character on your video display. When you are sending data to a remote computer, you may choose to have the remote computer display the characters on your display as a means of confirming that the remote system received the characters you sent. This kind of arrangement is called *full duplex*. If the other system is not able to send the characters back to you, you may choose simply to display the characters locally by choosing *half duplex.*

  If you are unsure of which option to select, begin typing. If your screen displays two of every character, then you should switch to full duplex. On the other hand, if you type characters and no characters are displayed on your screen, switch to half duplex.

- *Bits/Char:* Most systems communicate using 7 or 8 bits for each word. This is because ASCII code (the most common digital code for sending characters in personal computers) uses 7 bits per character. The eighth bit is often used as a parity bit. If you are unsure of the number of bits to use, consult the remote unit. If this is impractical, try 7 or 8 bits.

- *Strip Bit:* Systems will often include an extra bit as a buffer bit when they transmit. If the remote computer uses these, you will want to remove that bit from the data before you process it.

- *Flow Control:* These options relate to the two more common methods of serial *handshaking,* the process by which the two computers know when to send data and when to wait to receive it. Once again, it does not matter which method you use as long as the two systems use the same method.

Once you have made all of your selections, point the mouse pointer at the OK box to accept the changes (or the Cancel box to use the old settings) and click the left mouse button once.

A third option when the terminal screen appears is to press the UNDO key, which will cause you to exit the VT52 emulator.

CONTROL PANEL

If you select the item labeled "Control Panel" in the Desk menu, the ST will display the following window.

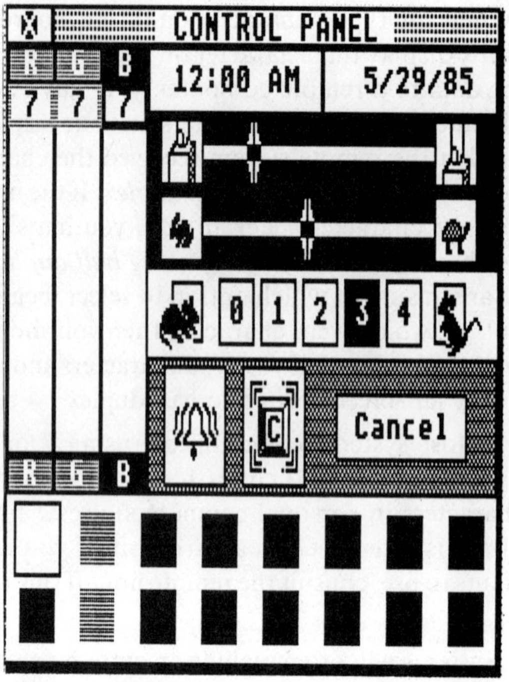

The Control Panel allows you to customize your ST so that it will best suit your needs. The options you can modify with the Control Panel are the clock, the calendar, keyboard sensitivity, mouse sensitivity, and screen color(s).

The ST does not have a battery-powered clock, so each time you turn it off, it loses track of the current time. Therefore, you may want to reset the time of day whenever you turn the computer on. To set the time, point to the clock display (in the center of the Control Panel just below the title bar) with the mouse pointer, and click the mouse button. When the clock is highlighted, simply type in the correct time.

The calendar is driven by the clock circuitry, so each time the ST is turned off, the date is lost as well. To set the date, select the Date box (just to the right of the Time box) and enter the date.

Everyone types differently, and most of us like a certain typewriter keyboard because of its "feel." While "feel" is partially controlled by the actual touch of the keys, it also consists of other factors that can be adjusted easily on the ST. The three factors you can adjust are the repeat rate, the repeat delay, and the key click.

If you hold down any character key on the keyboard for a few moments, that key will begin to repeat. To adjust the speed at which the keyboard generates repeat characters, position the mouse pointer on the slider that has a rabbit on the left and a turtle on the right. Move the slider left (for a faster repeat) or right (for a slower repeat).

To adjust the delay time between the keypress and the generation of repeat characters, move the slider with the finger/keytop at either end to the left (to shorten the delay) or to the right (to lengthen the delay).

Each time you click a mouse button, the ST waits for a short period to be sure that you are not going to double-click. Double-clicks have a special meaning to the ST and must be distinguished from single-clicks.

When you first use the mouse, you may find that you cannot click the mouse button quickly enough to produce reliable double-clicks when you need them. If this is the case, you can make the ST wait longer by clicking a smaller number in the boxes that lie between the alert mouse and the sleepy mouse near the center of the Control Panel. Of course, as you become more experienced, you may find the additional delay bothersome. To make the delay shorter, click the squares with larger numbers (the shortest delay is obtained by selecting the number 4).

Another keyboard option you may select is the key click. If you do not typically look at the screen, you may want to install key clicks as audible verification that the computer has accepted a keystroke. To turn on the key click, point at the symbol of a keytop (with the letter C in it) and click the mouse button. This will draw the symbol in black lines. (When the symbol is gray, it is disabled.)

In addition, you may want the ST to notify you of errors with a bell tone. To enable the error tone, click the symbol that looks like a small bell.

If you are using a color monitor, you can select the colors that the ST displays by selecting the various color patches at the bottom of the Control Panel. If you are in low-resolution mode, you will be able to select as many as 16 different colors. In high-resolution mode you will have 4 colors, and in monochrome mode you may toggle between standard and inverse video (black characters on a white background, and white characters on a black background).

To modify a color, click on its color patch and move the vertical R/G/B sliders up or down. For more color, move the slider up; for less, move it down.

SET RS232 CONFIG.

This sets all the RS232 configuration settings. It is the same control as that discussed earlier.

INSTALL PRINTER

The ST will work with the Atari SMM 804 monochrome printer or any Epson-like printer. The default values (with all of the left-hand selections highlighted) are set for the SMM 804. To use the color printer, switch the B/W-Color box to Color. To use an Epson or Epson-like printer, set the controls to

- Dot
- B/W
- 960 Pixels/Line
- Draft Quality
- Printer Port
- Feed Paper.

SET PREFERENCES

Select the Options menu and click on the Set Preferences option. This window allows you to make three choices:

- Confirm Deletes
- Confirm Copies
- Screen Resolution.

If you are a beginner, set the first two options to Yes. This will allow you to change your mind before the ST erases or copies any files.

The third option allows you to control the screen resolution if you have a color monitor. In low-resolution mode, the ST displays 320 horizontal dots by 200 vertical dots in 16 colors. In medium-resolution mode, the ST produces 640 dots by 200 dots in 4 colors. If you have a monochrome monitor, the ST will always display in high-resolution mode (630 dots by 400 dots).

PRINT SCREEN

The Print Screen function does just what it says: it prints the screen, exactly as it appears on the connected printer. Before you select this option, make sure that your printer is on and properly configured. If it is not, you may lock up the computer.

The remaining menu options on the desktop are housekeeping functions that we will discuss throughout the text of this book.

The remaining option that is not a housekeeping function is Save Desktop. This will save all of the modifications that you have made to your system through the Control Panel and the other menu controls. It will also save the current window size and location.

CHAPTER 3

An Introduction To LOGO

This chapter will teach you how to program your Atari 520-ST using LOGO, the language that is included with the computer. If you are already familiar with LOGO, Chapter 7 will serve as a comprehensive reference to each *primitive* (a built-in LOGO instruction that has a preprogrammed instruction) in the language. If you are a beginner, start with this chapter. It will give you the background necessary to continue through the rest of the book.

PREPARING FOR LOGO

Before you start LOGO, there is one more bit of preparation that you should perform: backing up the master disks that came with the computer. You have only one copy of each of these valuable program disks, and without the programs on these disks you will not be able to run the ST.

To back up your master disks, do the following:

1. Obtain two new 3 1/2-inch floppy disks
2. Insert the first new disk into drive A
3. Click on the drive A icon in the upper-right corner of the screen.

4. Select Format... from the File menu.

The following message box will appear:

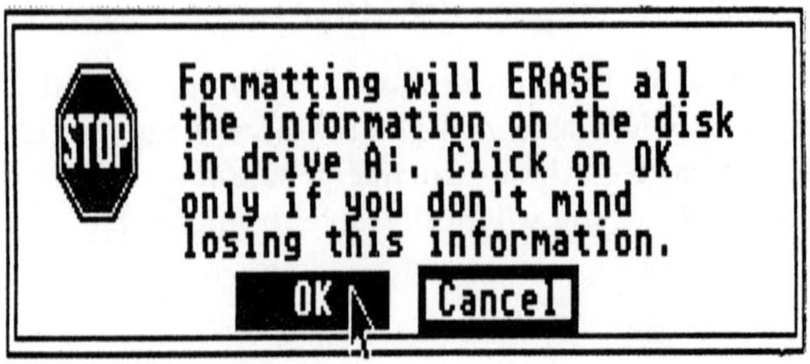

5. Click OK, and you will get another message box:

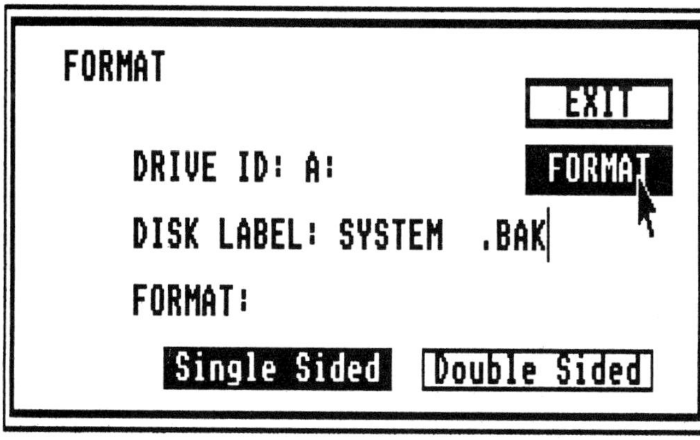

Name the first disk **SYSTEM.BAK**.

6. After you have entered the disk label, click in the box that contains the word "Format".
7. While the ST is formatting your disk, it will display the Format box:

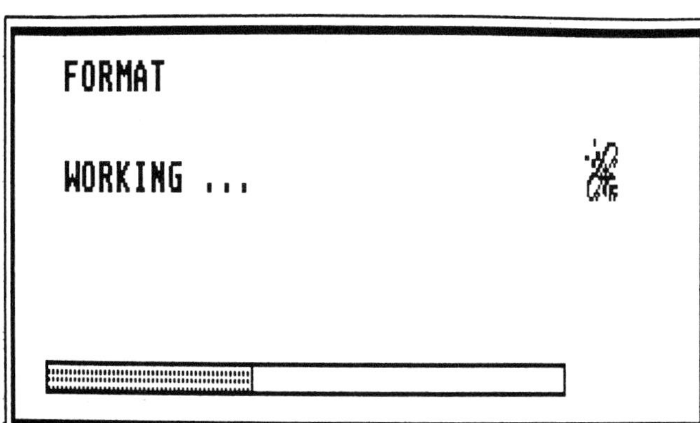

8. When formatting is complete, the ST will display the following box if formatting was successful.

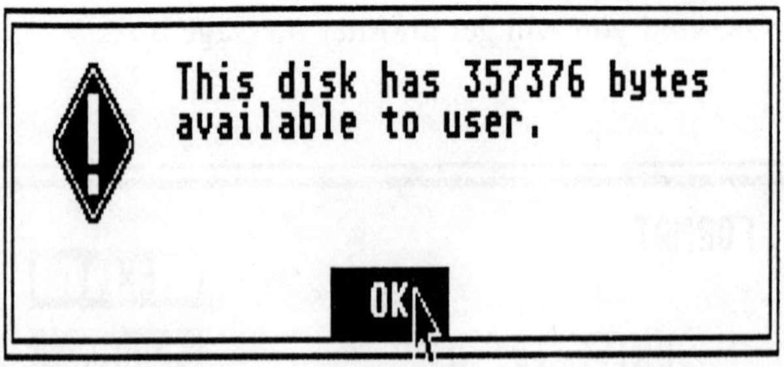

Click on the OK box, and you will return to the Format disk label box.

9. Use the backspace key to erase the label SYSTEM.BAK, and enter the name **LANGUAGE.BAK**.

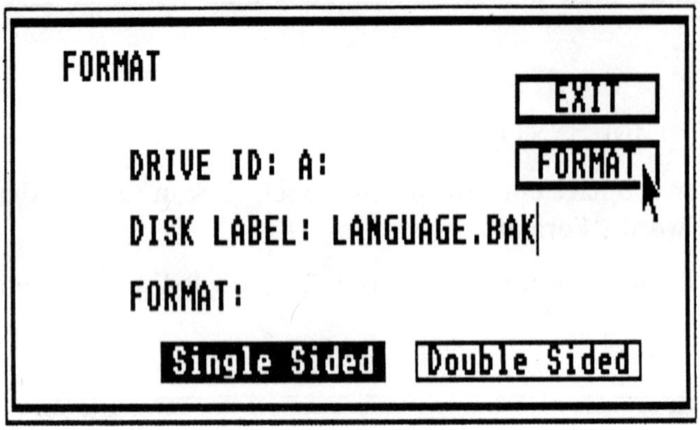

10. Eject the first disk, and insert the second disk into drive A.
11. Repeat steps 6 through 8; you will then have two formatted disks.
12. Click on the Exit box.

To copy the programs onto your new formatted disks, perform the following steps:

1. Hold the TOS system disk so that its label is up, the metal shutter is down, and so that you can see the round, metal disk hub in the center of the disk.

In the upper-left corner of the disk, you will find a small tab. This is the *write-protect slider.*

2. If the slider is in the lower position, slide it up into upper position. It should click in place.

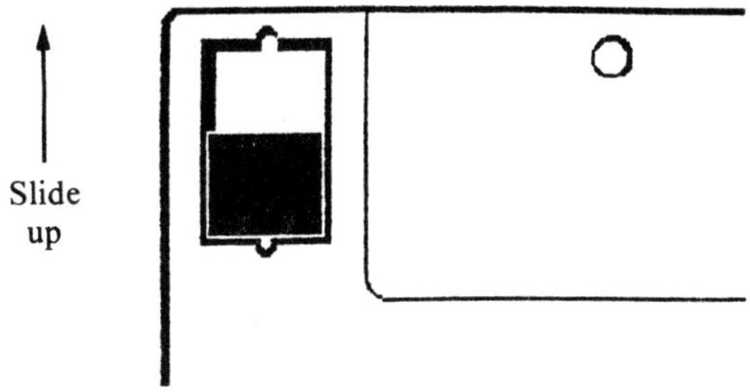

3. Repeat this for the LANGUAGE disk.

The next part of the procedure depends on how many disk drives you are using. If you have one disk drive, follow steps 4 through 9. If you have two disk drives, follow steps 10 through 14.

4. Insert the system disk into the disk drive.
5. Drag the drive A icon on top of the drive B icon.

FLOPPY DISK
FLOPPY DISK

The system will display the following message:

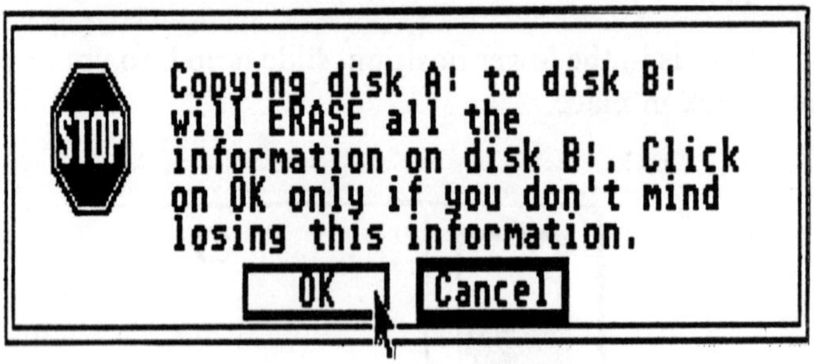
STOP
Copying disk A: to disk B: will ERASE all the information on disk B:. Click on OK only if you don't mind losing this information.
OK
Cancel

6. Click in the OK box, and you will get this message:

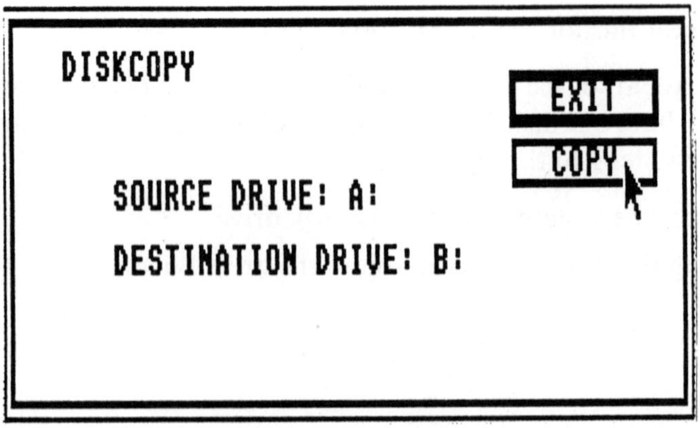
DISKCOPY
EXIT
COPY
SOURCE DRIVE: A:
DESTINATION DRIVE: B:

7. Click in the Copy box and you will be prompted to insert disk B into drive A.

Eject disk A, insert disk B, and click in the OK box.

8. After a few moments, you will be prompted to swap disks again. Throughout the copy process, swap disks as you are directed. While the disk is being copied, the ST will display the Diskcopy window.

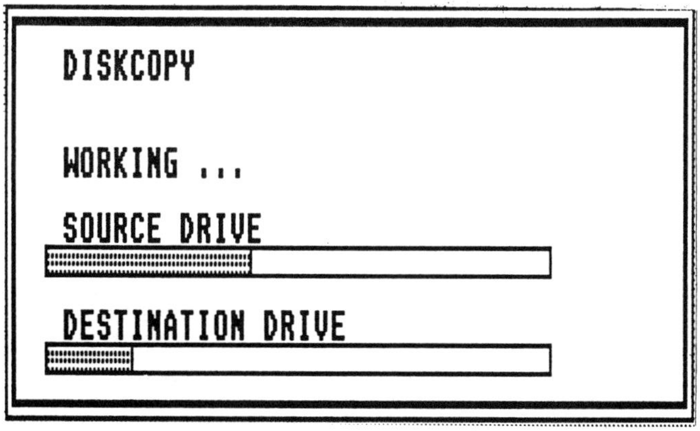

9. When the copy is complete, you will get the Copy's message box again. To make a copy of the LANGUAGE disk, insert that disk into drive A and click Copy again. This time, when you are prompted to insert disk B, insert the LANGUAGE.BAK disk (the other disk you formatted earlier).
10. If you have two disk drives, insert the system disk into drive A and the SYSTEM.BAK disk into drive B.
11. Drag the drive A icon on top of the drive B icon.

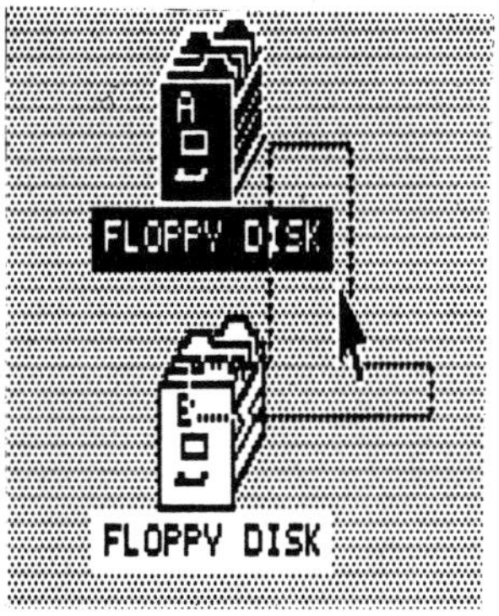

The system will display the following message:

STOP
Copying disk A: to disk B: will ERASE all the information on disk B:. Click on OK only if you don't mind losing this information.
OK
Cancel

12. Click in the OK box, and you will get this message:

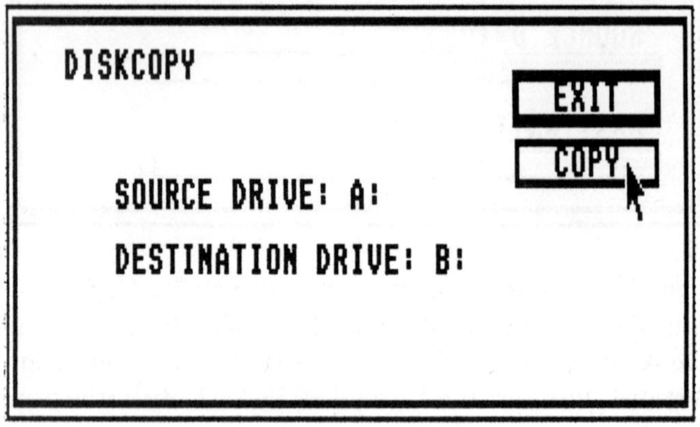

13. Click in the Copy box. While the disk is being copied, the ST will display the Diskcopy window.

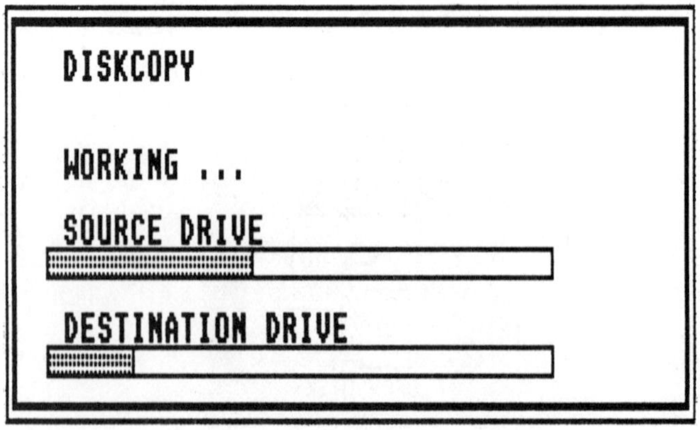

14. When the copy is complete, you will get the Copy message box again. To make a copy of the LANGUAGE disk, insert that disk into drive A and the LANGUAGE.BAK disk (the other disk you formatted earlier) into drive B.

Put the master disks in a safe place, away from heat, moisture, and magnetic fields. From this point on, always use the backup disks for any operations.

ELEMENTS OF A PROGRAMMING LANGUAGE

Program statements must be written following a well-defined set of rules. These rules, taken together, are referred to as *syntax*. There are many different sets of rules that define how program statements are written. Each set of rules applies to a different programming language. All of the syntax rules described in this book apply to Atari 520-ST LOGO.

Programming languages, like spoken languages, are varied. In addition to LOGO, there are many other programming languages, such as BASIC, Pascal, FORTRAN, COBOL, APL, PL/M, PL-1, and FORTH. Uncommon programming languages number in the hundreds.

Like spoken languages, programming languages have many dialects. A LOGO program written for the ST may not run on another computer, even if the other computer is programmable in LOGO. These variations in language syntax are due to different computers' various limitations or special features. However, having learned how to program your ST in LOGO, you will have little trouble learning other computers' LOGO dialects.

Some programming-language syntax rules are easy to understand. You do not have to be a programmer to understand the simple commands in Chapter 2. However, many syntax rules may seem arbitrary. For example, LOGO (and most other computing languages) uses the symbol * to represent multiplication. Why? One would normally use the × sign for multiplication, but a computer cannot differentiate between the use of the × sign to represent multiplication and its use to represent the letter X. Therefore, nearly all computer languages use the asterisk (*) to represent multiplication. Division is universally represented by a slash (/). Since the standard division sign is not present on computer or typewriter keyboards, the slash was selected, probably because it made the program expression look like a fraction.

LOGO programming syntax deals separately with single commands, primitives, procedures, and data. Each will be described in turn.

Starting LOGO

Before you can begin writing any LOGO programs, you will need to start the LOGO language program. To do this, insert the LANGUAGE disk into one of the disk drives and double-click that drive's icon. Next, point to the icon labeled LOGO.PRG and double-click again.

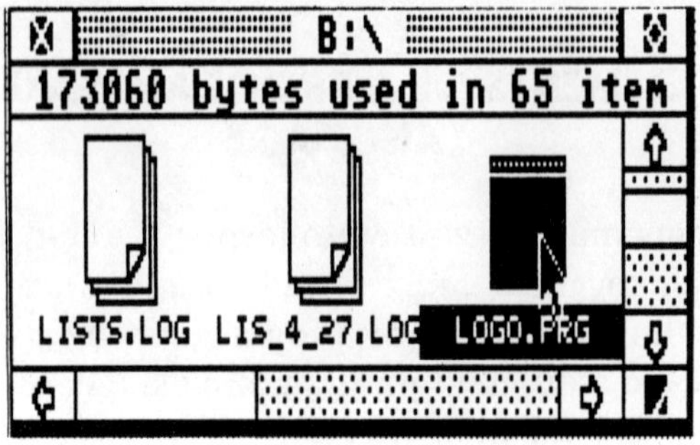

After a few moments, you will see the LOGO screen. The LOGO screen is initially divided into two windows: the LOGO Dialog window and the Graphics Display window (see Figure 3-1).

For the moment, you will not be using any graphics commands, so you can close the Graphics Display window. To close the window, position the mouse pointer anywhere inside the Graphics Display window and click the mouse button once. This will highlight the Graphics Display title and reveal its window controls. Point at the Close box (in the upper-left corner of the window) with the mouse pointer and click the mouse button once.

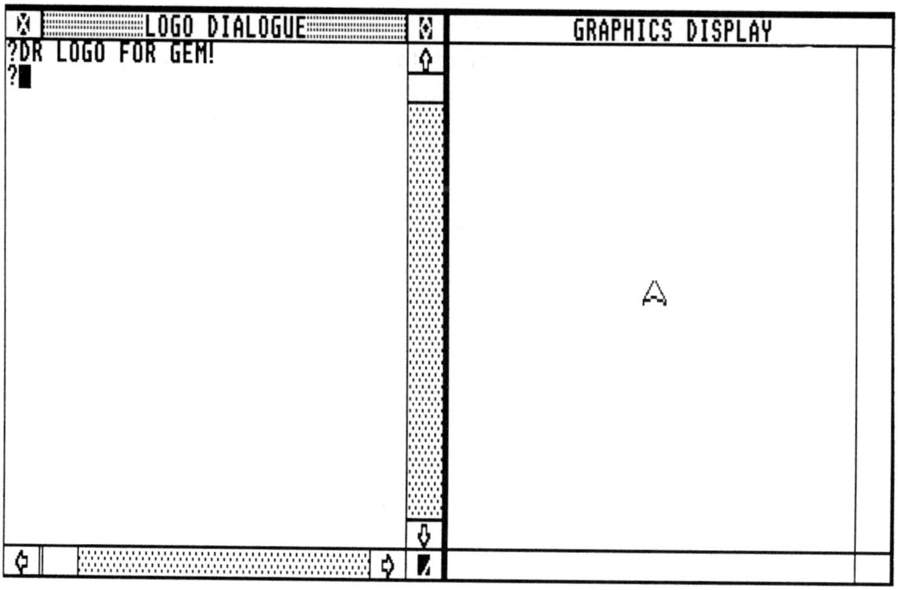

FIGURE 3-1. LOGO startup windows

Now point at the Settings menu and select the Close Edit option.

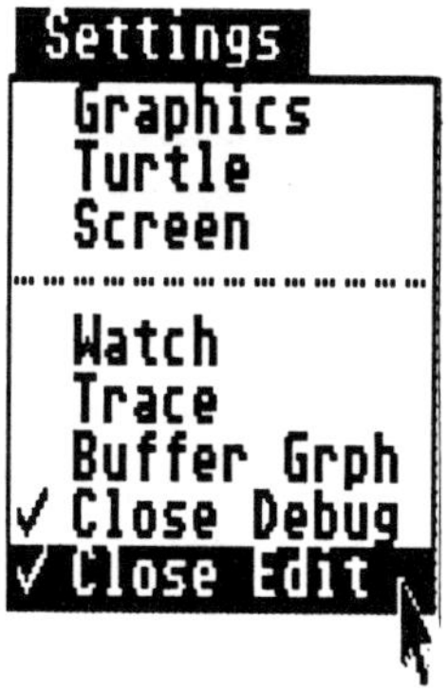

This will make the Edit window remain open all of the time. If this option is on (it has a check mark to its left in the menu), then the EDIT window will close each time you finish editing a procedure.

Select the Workspace option from the Edit menu. This will open the Edit window in the lower-left corner of the screen. Point the mouse pointer at the title bar, and drag the window up to the top of the screen (press and hold down the mouse button while you move the mouse up).

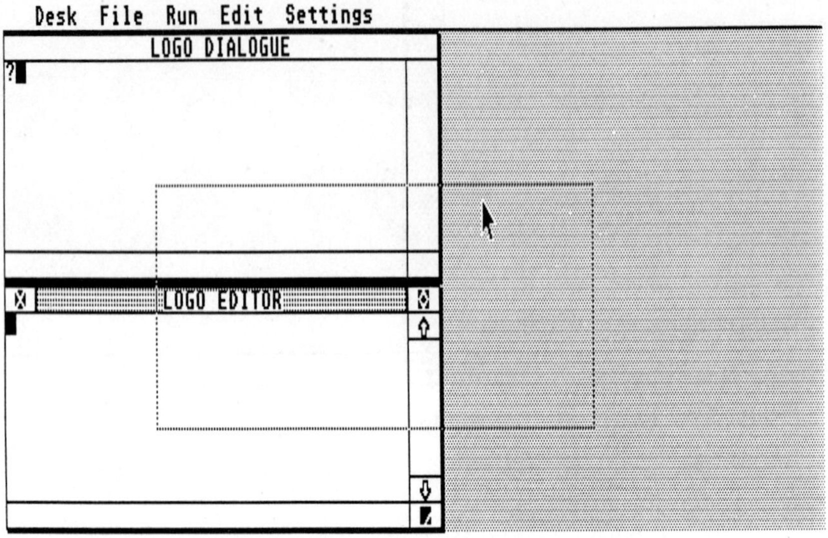

Now resize the Edit and Dialog windows with the Size boxes (in the lower-right corner of the window) to fill the screen as shown below:

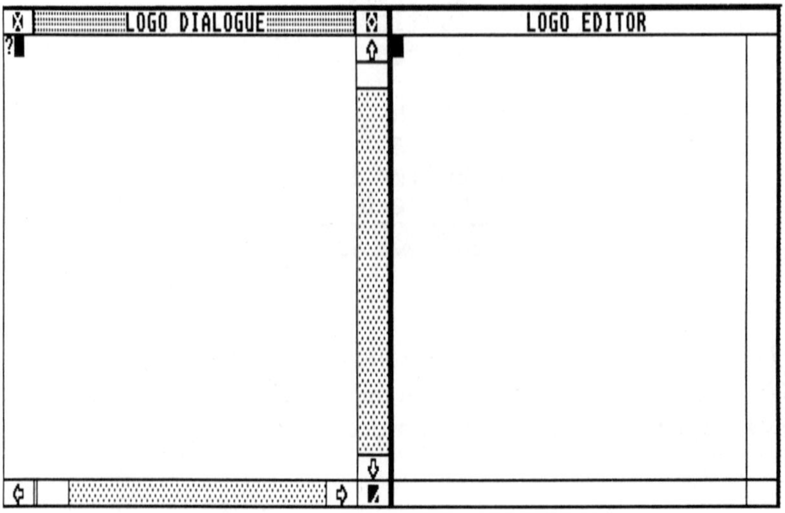

Immediate Mode

Find the cursor (the small, black rectangle) in the LOGO Dialog window. Directly to the left of the cursor you will find a question mark, which is the LOGO prompt. Whenever you see this prompt and the flashing cursor beside it, LOGO is waiting for you to enter something. In this section you'll look at the kinds of things LOGO expects you to enter.

The ST can execute two different kinds of instructions: *immediate* instructions and *programmed* instructions. Immediate instructions are executed as soon as they are typed into the computer, but programmed instructions are stored in memory until you run them.

In immediate mode, you can use the ST as you would a calculator. You simply enter *statements*—instructions to display information, perform a calculation, or carry out some other function. When you enter an immediate statement and press the RETURN key, the ST processes, or executes, the statement. First, however, the ST checks your entry for syntax. If the syntax is correct, the statement executes. If it isn't, you will get an error box describing the problem:

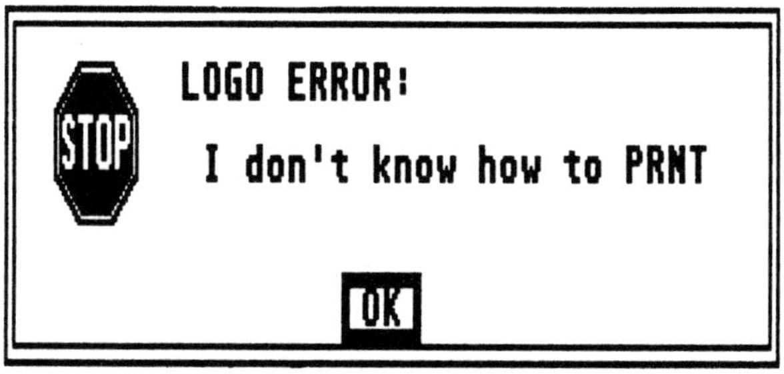
STOP
LOGO ERROR:
I don't know how to PRNT
OK

If you get an error message, check your statement for typographical errors.

The PRINT primitive is the most frequently used immediate-mode statement. As a primitive, it is a built-in instruction with a preprogrammed meaning. PRINT instructs the computer to display whatever follows it. For example, PRINT will display the results of a calculation such as this:

```
PRINT 1000 + 500 + 59
```

Enter the first line and LOGO will display the sum: 1559.

PRINT can also display individual characters or strings of characters (a *string* is a sequence of characters that can include letters, numbers, spaces, and symbols). To display a string like:

```
THE QUICK BROWN FOX
```

in the Dialog window, you could type the following immediate-mode statement:

```
PRINT [THE QUICK BROWN FOX]
```

The string is enclosed in brackets; anything enclosed in brackets in a PRINT statement will display literally as a string of characters.

For example, a PRINT statement such as

```
PRINT [4 + 8 + 16]
```

will not calculate anything. The computer will simply display the string of characters, which in this case is three numbers separated by plus signs. Conversely, the statement

```
PRINT AND MILES TO GO...
```

will cause an Error box. The syntax of a PRINT statement always expects numeric or string information to follow. The word "MILES" does not represent a number and is not in brackets, so the ST rejects the statement.

You can abbreviate PRINT by using the letters PR. Also, if you are executing in immediate mode exclusively, you can simply delete the PRINT command, and LOGO will assume PRINT.

Screen Editing

A powerful feature of ST LOGO is the LOGO Editor and the line editor. The key to using the ST's editing capabilities is the cursor. In the LOGO Editor window, you can move the cursor in four directions: up, down, left, and right. You can also insert or delete characters anywhere in the window, or even clear parts or all of the window using the editor's commands. In the Dialog window you can move, insert, or delete anywhere within the current line.

EDITING TEXT ON THE CURRENT DISPLAY LINE

Occasionally, you may notice mistakes on a line that you are entering. You can correct them by backspacing to the error and typing it correctly. For example,

```
OUR BUDGEY█
```

was intended to display as OUR BUDGET. You can change the Y to a T easily enough.

Type in this line and use the backspace or the DELETE key to position the cursor over the Y:

```
OUR BUDGE█
OUR BUDGET█
```

To change the Y to a T, simply type **T**. This replaces the old letter and moves the cursor one position to the right.

SHIFTING AND DELETING TEXT WITH THE DELETE KEY

In the following example, the word "GARDEN" is spelled with two R's. It will be necessary to delete one of the R's and to move the remaining text to the left to close up the extra space left by the R.

To do this, use the left-arrow key to position the cursor over the second D, and press the DELETE key once. This will erase the letter to the left of the cursor, deleting the R and shifting the text left one character to fill the space.

```
GARRDEN
GARDEN
```

INSERTING CHARACTERS

In the next example, we need to change "THE ENGINE" to "THE STEAM ENGINE". To do this, use the left-arrow key to position the cursor over the space between THE and ENGINE, and simply start typing. Each new letter you type will move the text to the right of the letter by one space.

```
THE█ENGINE
THE STEAM█ENGINE
```

Arithmetic Calculations

ST LOGO can perform the four standard mathematical operations: addition, subtraction, multiplication, and division. To multiply 4 by 4, you would enter

```
PRINT 4 * 4
```

To divide 8 by 2, you would enter:

```
PRINT 8 / 2
```

PROGRAM MODE

If you are familiar with the BASIC programming language, you are probably used to calling the instructions built into the programming language commands, statements, or functions. In other languages, the routines you write are called programs. In LOGO the built-in commands are called *primitives,* and the routines that you write are called *procedures.* The biggest advantage of using procedures (as you will see) is that once you have written a procedure, it can then be used like a primitive in building new procedures.

In both immediate mode and programmed mode, you enter statements and the computer responds to them. However, immediate-mode statements are temporary. When you press the RETURN key, your statement is executed once and then forgotten.

The immediate mode examples you entered earlier in this chapter were simple, one-line routines that did not do much. Once you become familiar with your computer, you will want to write procedures. LOGO procedures can be hundreds of statements long. The 520-ST stores program-mode statements in main memory.

Entering a Procedure

Procedures may be entered using the keyboard, or they can be loaded into memory through the disk drive. Each statement entered through the keyboard is stored in temporary memory when you enter it. Unless you specify otherwise, the lines in your programs will execute in the order in which they appear in the program.

Running a Program

Every procedure that you write must have a name. For example, enter this procedure:

```
TO CNT
MAKE "A 0
LABEL "LOOP
PRINT :A
MAKE "A :A + 1
GO "LOOP
END
```

To run the procedure, type its name and press RETURN:

```
?CNT
0
1
2
3
4
5
6
7
8
9
10
11
12
13
14
15
16
17
18
```

If you let it, this procedure will run forever. To end it, press the CONTROL key and the G key at the same time.

The GO in the sixth line tells the computer to return to the line with the label "CNT" and execute the instruction there.

When you type the procedure name, LOOP begins execution at the first line number in the procedure.

OPERATING THE DISK DRIVE

This section will cover the basic operation of the disk drive, listing the diskette directory, and loading and running programs from a diskette.

Loading a Procedure

There are two ways to load a procedure from a diskette in the disk drive. If you know the name of the file, give the LOAD command followed by the program name with a quote before it. For instance, if the name of the program is CNT, enter

```
LOAD "CNT
```

When the file has been loaded, LOGO will display each procedure in the file by name, followed by the word "defined" in the Dialog window. This means that LOGO now contains a definition for the procedure(s) you loaded. You may then either run the procedures or use them within other procedures.

If you are not sure of the exact name of a particular file or don't know what is on your diskette, pull down the File menu and select the Load option. This will display a window called the Item Selector, showing all the names of the files on the diskette.

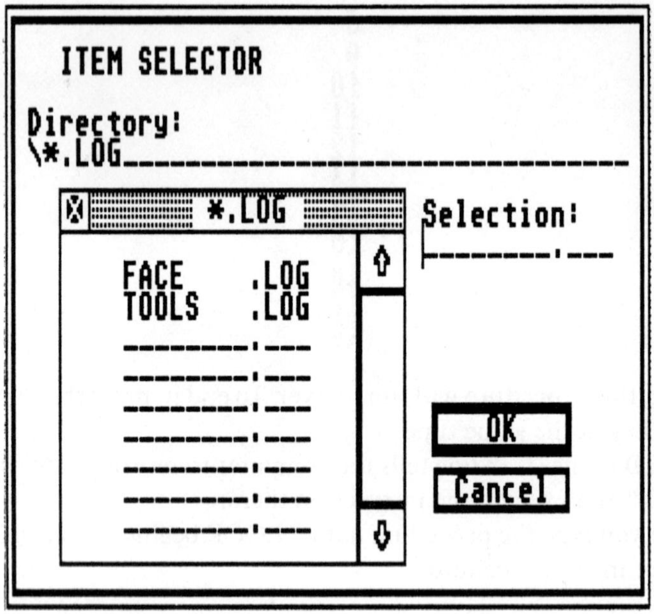

To load one of the listed files, you may either click on the file name and then click OK, or simply double-click the file name.

To recall any file from the diskette, it is absolutely necessary to enter the file name exactly as it is found on the disk. Therefore, it is generally easier to select files from the Item Selector window.

Saving a Procedure

Saving a procedure onto a diskette is nearly the same as loading a program. To save a procedure on diskette, type the command

```
SAVE "CNT
```

If you only have one disk drive, you do not need to include the drive letter. After you press RETURN, the disk drive should activate, the red light on its front should light, and the cursor should disappear. After the program has been saved, the screen will show the "?" prompt, and the cursor will return.

THE LOGO LANGUAGE

The remainder of this chapter will discuss elements that you will need to know to use the LOGO language—from numbers and strings to functions.

Numbers

LOGO can work with numbers represented in three different ways: as integers, floating points, and scientific notation. An integer is a number that has no fraction or decimal point. The number can be negative (−) or positive (+). An unsigned number is assumed to be positive. Any integer can also be represented as a floating-point number, since integers are a subset of floating-point numbers.

Strings

The word *string* is used to describe data that consists of characters. This includes any non-numeric data.

You have already used strings as messages to be displayed on the ST's screen. A string consists of one or more characters enclosed in brackets or preceded by a quotation mark:

```
[THIS IS A STRING]

"STRING
```

Within a string you can include alphabetic or numeric characters, special symbols, or graphics characters.

Variables

Consider the following LOGO command:

```
MAKE "A :C + :B
```

This displays the sum of two numbers. The two numbers are whatever B and

C represent at the time the statements are executed. In the following example

```
TO EXAMPLE
MAKE "B 4.65
MAKE "C 3.27
MAKE "A :B + :C
PRINT :A
END
```

B is assigned the value 4.65, while C is assigned the value 3.27. Therefore A equals 7.92.

Variable Names

Variable names can be used to represent string data or numeric data. If you have studied elementary algebra, you will have no trouble understanding the concept of variables and variable names. If you have never studied algebra, then think of a variable name as a name that is assigned to a mailbox. Anything that is placed in the mailbox becomes the value associated with the mailbox's name.

As shown in the preceding examples, one way that LOGO assigns variable names is with the primitive called MAKE. For example,

```
MAKE "A 10
```

assigns the value 10 to the variable A. If you want LOGO to display the value of A, type

```
PRINT :A
```

and press RETURN.

Notice that you use a quotation mark to assign the variable and a colon to recall it.

NOTE: If the string begins with a number, it will be treated as a number, not as a character, even if you use quotes.

Operators

The LOGO statement

```
PRINT 10.2 + 4.7
```

tells the ST to add 10.2 and 4.7, and then display the sum. The statement

```
MAKE "C :A + :B
```

tells the ST to add the two numbers represented by the variable names A and

B, and to assign the sum to the number represented by the variable name C.

The plus sign specifies addition and is referred to as an *arithmetic* operator. There are two other types of operators: *relational* and *Boolean* operators. These take a little more explanation, since they reflect conditions and decisions, rather than arithmetic.

Table 3-1 summarizes the LOGO operators. We will examine each group of operators in turn, beginning with arithmetic operators.

Arithmetic Operators

An arithmetic operator specifies addition, subtraction, multiplication, division, or exponentiation. Arithmetic operations are performed using floating-point numbers. Integers are automatically converted to floating-point numbers before an arithmetic operation is performed, and the result is automatically converted back to an integer if an integer variable represents the result.

The data operated on by any operator is referred to as an *operand*. Arithmetic operators each require two operands, which may be numbers, numeric variables, or a combination of both.

TABLE 3-1. Operators

	Precedence	Operator	Meaning
	High 9	( )	Parentheses denote order of evaluation
Arithmetic Operators	8	^	Exponentiation
	7	—	Unary minus
	6	*	Multiplication
	6	/	Division
	5	+	Addition
	5	—	Subtraction
Relational Operators	4	=	Equal
	4	<>	Not equal
	4	<	Less than
	4	>	Greater than
	4	<= or =<	Less than or equal
	4	>= or =>	Greater than or equal
Boolean Operators	3	NOT	Logical complement
	2	AND	Logical AND
	1 Low	OR	Logical OR

ADDITION (+)

The plus sign specifies that the data (or operand) on the left of the plus sign is to be added to the data (or operand) on the right. For numeric quantities, this is straightforward addition.

SUBTRACTION (−)

The minus sign specifies that the operand on the right of the minus sign is to be subtracted from the operand on the left of the minus sign. For example,

```
4-1       results in 3
100-64    results in 36
A-B       results in the variable
            represented by label B
            being subtracted from the
            variable represented by
            label A
55-142    results in -87
```

The minus operator also identifies a negative number. For example,

```
-5
-9E4
-B
4--2          Note that 4 -- 2 is the same as 4+2
```

MULTIPLICATION (*)

An asterisk specifies that the operand on the right of the asterisk is to be multiplied by the operand on the left of the asterisk. For example,

```
100 * 2      results in 200
50 * 0       results in 0
A * X1       results in multiplication of
               two floating point numbers
               represented by floating point
               variables labeled A and X1
R% * 14      results in an integer
               represented by integer variable
               label R% being multiplied by 14
```

DIVISION (/)

The slash specifies that the operand on the left of the slash is to be divided by the data (or operand) on the right of the slash, shown as follows.

10/2	results in 5
6400/4	results in 1600
A/B	results in the floating point number assigned to variable A being divided by the floating point number assigned to variable B
4E2/XR	results in 400 being divided by the floating point number represented by label XR

EXPONENTIATION (^)

The caret specifies that the operand on the left of the arrow is raised to the power specified by the operand on the right of the arrow. If the operand on the right is 2, the number on the left is squared; if the operand on the right is 3, the number on the left is cubed, and so on. The exponent can be any number, variable, or expression. For example,

2^2	results in 4
12^2	results in 144
1^3	results in 1
A^5	results in the floating point number assigned to variable A being raised to the 5th power
2^6.4	results in 84.4485064
NM^−10	results in the floating point number assigned to variable NM being raised to the negative 10th power
14^F	results in 14 being raised to the power specified by floating point variable F

ORDER OF EVALUATION

An expression may have several arithmetic operations, as in the following statement:

```
?PRINT 4 + 5 * 10
54
```

When this occurs, there is a fixed sequence in which operations are processed (this was shown in Table 3-1). First comes exponentiation, followed by sign evaluation, followed by multiplication and division, and then by addition and subtraction. Operations of equal precedence are evaluated from left to right. This order of operation can be overridden by the use of parentheses. Any operation within parentheses is performed first. Here is an example:

```
?PRINT (4 + 5) * 10
90
```

When parentheses are present, LOGO evaluates the innermost set first, then the next innermost, and so on. Parentheses can be nested to any level and may be used freely to clarify the order of operations being performed in an expression.

Relational Operators

Relational operators represent the following conditions: greater than (>), less than (<), equal (=), not equal (<>), greater than or equal (>=), and less than or equal (<=).

1=5−4	results in TRUE
14>66	results in FALSE
15> =15	results in TRUE
A<>B	the result will depend on the values assigned to variables A and B

Relational operators can be used to compare strings; for example, the letters of the alphabet have the order “A<”B, “B<”C, “C<”D, and so on. Strings are compared one character at a time, starting with the leftmost character.

When operating on strings, LOGO generates the words TRUE for a “true” result, and FALSE for a “false” result:

Boolean Operators

Boolean operators give programs the ability to make decisions based on choices. There are three Boolean operators in LOGO: AND, OR, and NOT.

A simple supermarket-shopping analogy can serve to illustrate Boolean logic. Suppose you are shopping for breakfast cereals with two children. The AND Boolean operator says that a cereal is selected only if child A and child B select the cereal. The OR Boolean operator says that a cereal will be selected

TABLE 3-2. Boolean Truth Table

The AND operation results in a TRUE only if both values are TRUE:
AND (1 = 1) (2 = 2) TRUE
AND (1 = 0) (2 = 2) FALSE
AND (0 = 0) (1 = 2) FALSE
AND (1 = 0) (1 = 0) FALSE

The OR operation results in a 1 if either number is 1:
AND (1 = 1) (2 = 2) TRUE
AND (1 = 0) (2 = 2) TRUE
AND (0 = 0) (1 = 2) TRUE
AND (1 = 0) (1 = 0) FALSE

The NOT operation logically complements each number:
NOT 1 = 0 TRUE
NOT 0 = 0 FALSE

if either child A or child B selects the cereal. The NOT operator generates a logical opposite. If child B insists on disagreeing with child A, then child B's decision is always not child A's decision.

Table 3-2 summarizes the way in which Boolean operators handle numbers. This table is referred to as a *truth table.*

Reserved Words

All of the character combinations that define a LOGO primitive's operations, and all functions, are called *reserved words.* Table 3-3 lists the 520-ST LOGO reserved words. You will encounter some of these reserved words in this chapter, and others are described in later chapters.

When executing LOGO procedures, the ST scans every LOGO statement, seeking out any character combinations that make up reserved words. The only exception is text strings enclosed in brackets. This can cause you trouble if a reserved word is embedded anywhere within a variable name. The ST cannot identify a variable name by its location in a statement. Therefore, you need to be very careful to keep reserved words out of your variable names. This is particularly important with the short reserved words that can easily slip into variable names.

TABLE 3-3. LOGO Primitive Abbreviations

PRIMITIVE	ABBREVIATION	PRIMITIVE	ABBREVIATION
BACK	BK	PENDOWN	PD
BUTFIRST	BF	PENERASE	PE
BUTLAST	BL	PENREVERSE	PX
CLEARSCREEN	CS	PENUP	PU
CLEARTEXT	CT	PRINT	PR
EDIT	ED	READCHAR	RC
ERASE	ER	READLIST	RL
FORWARD	FD	READQUOTE	RQ
HIDETURTLE	HT	RIGHT	RT
IFFALSE	IFF	SCREENFACTS	SF
IFTRUE	IFT	SENTENCE	SE
LEFT	LT	SETHEADING	SETH
LOWERCASE	LC	SHOWTURTLE	ST
OUTPUT	OP	TURTLEFACTS	TF
PALETTE	PAL	TURTLETEXT	TT

LOGO Primitive Abbreviations

You learned early in this book that the LOGO statement PRINT could always be entered from the keyboard by the abbreviation "PR." Many LOGO primitives can be abbreviated, as shown in Table 3-3.

LOGO Primitives

The operation performed by a procedure is specified using primitives of their abbreviations. Primitives are not described in detail in this chapter. This chapter introduces you to programming concepts, stressing the way primitives are used.

Remarks

If the first character of a LOGO statement is a semicolon, the computer ignores the statement entirely. You should include such statements because remarks make your program easier to read.

If you write a short program with five or ten statements, you will probably have little trouble remembering what the program does—unless you leave it around for six months and then try to use it again. On the other hand, if you write a longer program with perhaps 100 or 200 statements, you are quite likely to forget something very important the very next time you use the program. After you have written dozens of programs, you cannot possibly remember each one in detail. The solution to this problem is to document your program by including remarks that describe what the various parts of the program do.

It is good practice to use plenty of remarks in your programs. In all of the longer program examples in this book, we will include remarks that describe what is going on, simply to get you into the habit of doing the same thing yourself.

Branch Statements

Statements within a LOGO program normally execute in the order in which they appeared within a procedure. Branch statements such as GO can change this execution sequence.

GO

Ordinarily, procedures are executed one at a time from the top of your program, in the order they appear. GO tells the ST to branch to a statement out of order. It allows you to specify the statement that will be executed next. Consider the following example:

```
TO LOOPTEST
MAKE "A 4.37
GO "LOOP
.
.
.
.
.
LABEL "LOOP
.
.
.
END
```

The second statement is an assignment statement; it assigns a value to the variable A. The next statement is a GO statement; it specifies that program execution must branch to the tenth line (labeled LOOP). Therefore, the instruction execution sequence surrounding this part of the program will be the second line, then the third line, and then the tenth line.

You can branch to any line, even if the line has nothing but a comment on it. However, the computer ignores the comment so the effect is the same as branching to the next line. For example, consider the following branch:

```
TO LOOPTEST
MAKE "A 4.37
GO "LOOP
.
.
.
.
.
LABEL "LOOP
; --- THIS IS A COMMENT LINE ---
.
.
END
```

REPEAT COMMAND

The GO statement lets you create any type of statement-execution sequence that your program logic requires. But suppose you want to reexecute an instruction (or a group of instructions) many times. For example, suppose you want your program to count from 1 to 100. Should you use a GO command 100 times? Writing a hundred GO statements would be tedious. It is far simpler to reexecute one statement 100 times. There are several ways you can accomplish this, but the easiest is to use the REPEAT command; for instance:

```
TO CNT
MAKE "A 0
REPEAT 100 [PRINT :A MAKE "A :A + 1]
END
```

Nested Loops

The REPEAT and GO structures are referred to as program *loops,* since statement execution loops through the same series of commands many times. This loop structure is very common; almost every LOGO program that you write will include one or more loops. Loops are so common that they are frequently nested. The statement sequence occurring between the beginning and the end of a loop can be of any length; it can run to tens or even hundreds of statements. And within these tens or hundreds of statements, additional loops may occur.

Subprocedures And Superprocedures

Once you start writing programs that are more than a few statements long, you will quickly find short procedures that you use repeatedly. For example, suppose you have a variable (such as A) that is reinitialized frequently at different points in your program. Would you simply repeat the three instructions that constitute the GO loop described earlier? Since there are only three instructions, you may as well do so.

Suppose, however, you have to initialize some variables and then execute 10 or 15 instructions that process data in some fashion. If you had to use this loop many times within one program, rewriting 10 to 15 statements each time you wished to use it would take time, but more importantly, it would waste a good deal of computer memory. This can be illustrated as follows:

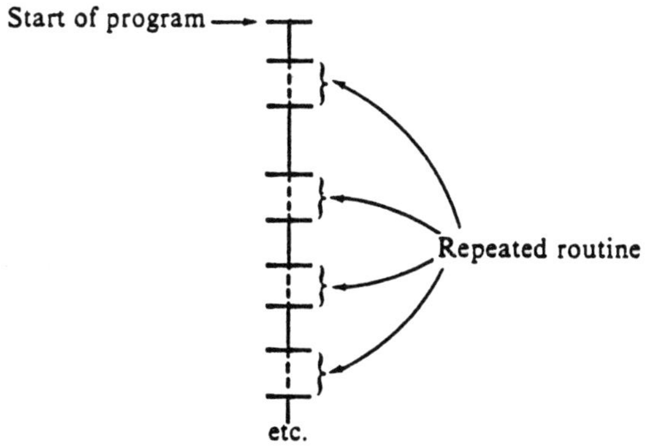

To solve this problem, you can separate out the repeated statements and branch to them many times. We'll refer to this group of statements as a *subprocedure,* and we'll call the procedure that utilizes one or more of these subprocedures a *superprocedure.*

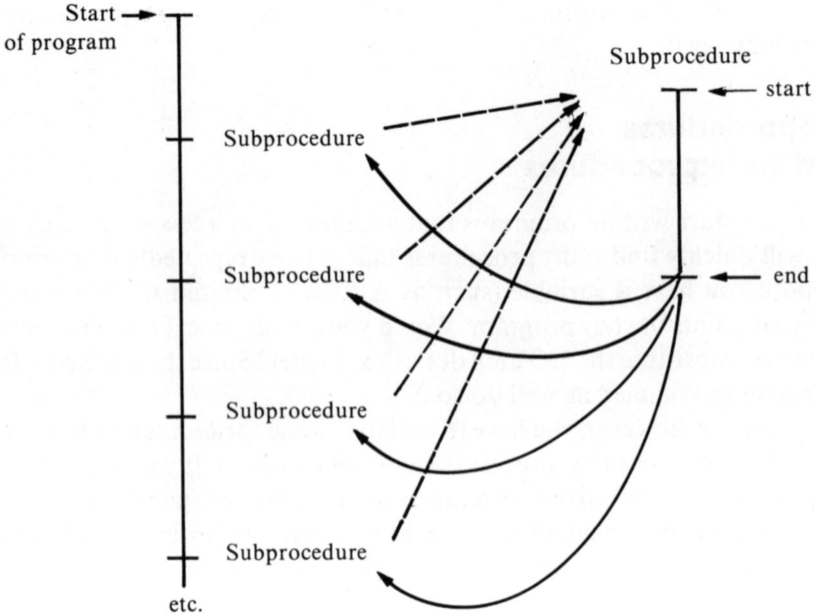

IF Statement

The arithmetic and relational operators described earlier in this chapter are frequently used in IF statements. This gives a LOGO program decision-making capabilities. Following the IF statement you enter any expression. If the expression is true, the statements following the IF are executed; however, if the expression is false, the statements are not executed and the program moves on to the next instruction. Here are three simple examples of IF statements:

```
IF :A = :B + 5 [PRINT MSG1]
IF :CC<"M [MAKE "IN 0]
IF (AND (:Q < 14) (:M <> :M1)) [GO "LOOP]
```

The statement on the first line causes a PRINT statement to be executed if the value of variable A is five more than the value of variable B. The PRINT statement will not be executed otherwise. The statement on the next line sets the variable N to 0 if variable C is any letter of the alphabet in the range A though L. The statement on the third line causes program execution to branch to “LOOP if variable Q is less than 14 and variable M is not equal to variable M1.

Input/Output

There are a variety of LOGO statements that control the transfer of data to and from the computer. These are referred to as *input/output* statements. The simplest input/output statements control data input from the keyboard and data output to the display. There are also more complex input/output statements that control data transfer between the computer and such peripheral devices as disk drives and printers.

Earlier, we saw how to use the word PRINT, or its abbreviation PR, to create a PRINT statement. The PRINT statement will display any data. Text must be preceded by a quote. For example, the following statement will display the single word TEXT:

```
PRINT "TEXT
```

To display a number, you place that number or a variable name after PRINT.

You can display any mixture of text and numbers by enclosing information to be displayed by PRINT in brackets. The following PRINT statement displays the words "ONE," "TWO," "THREE," "FOUR," and "FIVE," followed by the numeral for each number:

```
?PRINT [ONE 1 TWO 2 THREE 3 FOUR 4 FIVE 5]
ONE 1 TWO 2 THREE 3 FOUR 4 FIVE 5
```

Notice that each item enclosed within the brackets is printed on the same line and is separated by a single space from the word before and after it. If you do not enclose the elements you want to print inside brackets but use quotes instead, PRINT will place each item on a separate line:

```
?PRINT "ONE "1 "TWO "2 "THREE "3 "FOUR "4 "FIVE "5
ONE
1
TWO
2
THREE
3
FOUR
4
FIVE
5
```

TYPE

The PRINT statement always automatically advances to the next line of the display. To "print" the items on the same line without the spaces between them, use the TYPE command instead of PRINT. To illustrate this, enter and run the program shown on the next page.

```
?PRINT "ONE "TWO
ONE
TWO
?
?TYPE "ONE "TWO
ONETWO
```

DISPLAYING VARIABLES

You have been illustrating the numerals by inserting them directly into the PRINT and TYPE statements. You can, if you wish, display the contents of variables instead. The following program uses the variable :A to create digits. Try entering and running this program:

```
?MAKE "A 20
?MAKE "B 30
?PRINT :A :B
20
30
?TYPE :A :B
2030
```

You can also use the PRINT and TYPE commands to perform mathematical operations. For example,

```
?PRINT 44 + 30
74
?TYPE 200 + 10
210
```

Input Statements

By this time you are probably quite used to entering information on the keyboard and having the ST respond to your entries. While you are inside a program, however, the ST will not normally be looking at the keyboard for information. You will need input statements to tell the computer when to look for information from the keyboard. ST LOGO has three kinds of input statements: READLIST, READQUOTE, and READCHAR. These allow you to enter information into a program while it is running.

READLIST AND READQUOTE

When a READLIST or READQUOTE statement is executed, the computer waits for input from the keyboard; until the computer receives this input, nothing else will happen.

A READLIST or READQUOTE statement usually begins with the word MAKE and a variable name. Entered data is assigned to the named variable. To demonstrate keyboard input, enter the following short program and run it:

```
TO READ_STUFF
MAKE "A READLIST
TYPE [YOU ENTERED:]
PRINT :A
END
```

Upon executing a READLIST or READQUOTE statement, the computer simply stops the program and waits for your entry. When you run the program, the cursor will appear on a blank. Type in a string and press RETURN; the program will continue.

As you can see, this program allows you to enter keyboard information into a program, but if you did not know that you were supposed to enter something, you would probably not do so, since the computer does not prompt you.

Here is the same program with a prompt that asks you to enter your name:

```
TO READ_STUFF2
PRINT [PLEASE ENTER YOUR NAME...]
MAKE "A READLIST
TYPE [YOU ENTERED:]
PRINT :A
END
```

By tailoring your prompts, you can lead the user through your program and get exactly the information needed.

READCHAR

The READCHAR statement lets you input a single character. No RETURN is needed. The input can be any character on the ST's keyboard; for example:

```
TO READ_STUFF3
PRINT [PLEASE ENTER ANY CHARACTER...]
MAKE "A READCHAR
TYPE [YOU ENTERED:]
PRINT :A
END
```

Arithmetic Functions

Table 3-4 is a list of the arithmetic functions that can be used with ST LOGO. The following example uses an arithmetic function:

```
TO EXAMPLE2
MAKE "A 2.743
MAKE "B ( INT :A) + 7
PRINT :A
END
```

TABLE 3-4. Arithmetic Functions

Function	Definition
ABS	Returns the absolute value of an argument. A positive argument does not change; a negative argument is converted to its positive equivalent.
ARCTAN	Returns the trigonometric arctangent of the argument in radians.
COS	Returns the trigonometric cosine of the argument in radians.
DEGREES	Converts an argument from radians to degrees.
EXP	Raises the natural logarithm base *e* to the power of the argument (e_{arg}).
INT	Converts a floating point argument to its integer equivalent by truncation.
LOG	Returns the natural logarithm of the argument.
LOG10	Returns the base 10 common logarithm of the argument.
PI	Returns the value of PI: 3.141592
PRODUCT	Returns the product of the two input arguments.
QUOTIENT	Returns the quotient of the two input arguments.
RADIANS	Converts an argument from degrees to radians.
RANDOM	Generates a random number. There are some rules regarding the use of random numbers; they are described in Chapter 4.
REMAINDER	Returns the integer remainder derived from the division of two arguments.
RERANDOM	Generates a repeatable random-number sequence.
ROUND	Similar to the INT function, but creates an integer by rounding off the decimal portion of the argument instead of truncating.
SIN	Returns the trigonometric sine of the argument in radians.

When you execute this program, the result displayed is 9, since the integer value of A is 2.

String Functions

String functions allow you to manipulate string data in a variety of ways. Table 3-5 lists the string functions that can be used with ST LOGO. String

TABLE 3-5. String Functions

FUNCTION	DEFINITION
ASCII	Returns the ASCII value of the argument.
BUTFIRST	Returns the entire string minus the first character.
BUTLAST	Returns the entire string minus the last character.
CHAR	Returns the ASCII character of the argument.
COUNT	Returns the number of items in the argument.
EMPTYP	True if the argument is undefined or empty.
EQUALP	True if the two input arguments are equal.
FIRST	Returns the first character of the argument.
FPUT	Combines the two input arguments, placing the first argument at the beginning of the resulting string.
ITEM	Returns the selected item of an argument.
LAST	Returns the last character of an argument.
LISTP	True if the input argument is a list.
LOWERCASE	Returns the argument in all lowercase letters.
LPUT	Combines the two input arguments, placing the first argument at the end of the resulting string.
MEMBERP	True if the first argument is a subset of the second argument.
PIECE	Returns the selected portion of an argument.
SENTENCE	Returns a list consisting of all the input arguments.
SORT	Returns a list of all input arguments rearranged in alphabetical order.
SQRT	Computes the square root of the argument.
SUM	Computes the sum of the input arguments.
TAN	Returns the trigonometric tangent of the argument in radians.
UPPERCASE	Returns the argument in all uppercase letters.
WORD	Produces a single word from all input arguments.

functions let you determine the length of a string, extract portions of a string, and convert between numeric, ASCII, and string characters. These functions take one, two, or three arguments. Here are some examples:

```
?ASCII "ANTS
65
?BUTFIRST "QUAIL
UAIL
?
?ITEM 1 "DOORKNOB
D
?
?LPUT "BIRTHDAY "HAPPY
HAPPYBIRTHDAY
?
```

CHAPTER

4 Advanced LOGO Programming

Although the previous chapter covered some of the inner workings of 520-ST LOGO, you will find that there is much more to be learned about programming. Whereas Chapter 3 covered the language itself, this chapter and those that follow will provide programming techniques and hints that will help you get the most out of your 520-ST.

Because this chapter concerns itself with more advanced programming, the program examples and explanations will be longer. You will probably want to enter and run each example in order to better understand the concepts being discussed.

Many of the program examples given in this chapter are designed for use in programs that you write yourself. Some are written as subprocedures and are designed to be used as parts of superprocedures.

THE BASICS

Before we begin this chapter, there are two operations that you should really understand: editing your procedures and listing your procedures.

To edit a procedure, type the word EDIT, a space, a single quote, and then the name of the procedure you want to edit. For example, to edit a procedure called TEST, you would enter **EDIT "TEXT**.

When you finish editing a procedure, press CONTROL-C to save the changes you just made. Typing CONTROL-G will discard your changes.

LOGO has several commands that will list procedures and variable values that are stored in memory, but the easiest command you can use to list the contents of the working memory is POALL. This lists everything that is currently in memory, including current variable values. If you use this command all of the time, you will always know what is being stored in a disk file when you save it.

In the examples and listings shown in this chapter, many of the listings will show the procedure and the values of the variables after running the procedure.

PROGRAMMING WITH STRINGS

In LOGO a string is any group of characters, including letters, numbers and many symbols. Strings can contain alphabetic characters, numeric characters, or combinations of both. You will find throughout this book that strings are described as *sentences*, *words*, and *lists*. Sentences are groups of words, words are groups of individual characters, and lists are any combination of these.

Concatenating Strings

It is useful to link shorter strings end-to-end in a chain-like fashion to create one large string. This linking process is called *concatenation*.

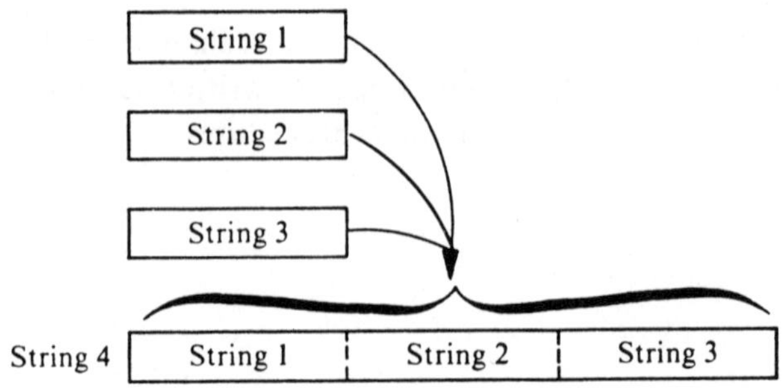

Suppose, for example, you want to create one large string, "Z, containing the alphabet. To do this, you would link the last character of "A (shown below) to the first character of "J, and the last character of "J to the first character of "S.

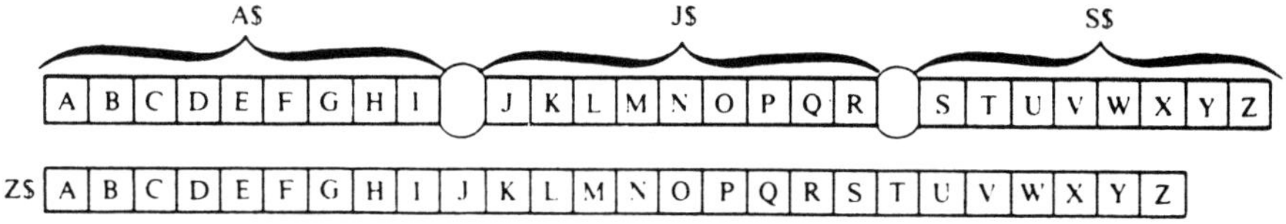

LPUT AND FPUT

LOGO offers a number of ways to put strings together. For example, one way to concantenate two strings is with the FPUT and LPUT primitives. FPUT takes the first string and places it in front of the second string. Here is an example:

```
MAKE "A "ABCDEFGHI
MAKE "J "JKLMNOPQR
MAKE "X FPUT :A :J
PRINT :X
```

LPUT does the opposite—it puts the second string in front of the first:

```
MAKE "A "ABCDEFGHI
MAKE "J "JKLMNOPQR
MAKE "X LPUT :J :A
PRINT :X
```

WORD AND SENTENCE

Another way you can concatenate strings is to use the primitives WORD and SENTENCE. WORD changes strings into a single word that is made up of the strings in the same order in which they appeared in the command, with no spaces between the strings.

```
MAKE "A "ABCDEFGHI
MAKE "J "JKLMNOPQR
MAKE "X WORD :A :J
PRINT :X
```

The SENTENCE primitive puts strings together and adds a single space between each of them. This allows you to easily separate the strings later should it be necessary.

```
MAKE "A "ABCDEFGHI
MAKE "J "JKLMNOPQR
MAKE "X SENTENCE :A :J
PRINT :X
```

Separating Strings

The correct way to extract or select part of a larger string is to use the string functions. These are FIRST, LAST, BUTFIRST, BUTLAST, ITEM, and PIECE. Since there are so many of these, they will be easier to learn if you examine each of them individually.

FIRST

The FIRST primitive returns the first item in a string or list. If FIRST is used with a string or a word, it will return the first character of the string or word, as in

```
MAKE "A "ABCDEFGHI
MAKE "B FIRST :A
PRINT :B
```

If FIRST is used with a list or sentence, it will return the first whole string in the list or sentence:

```
MAKE "A "HELLO
MAKE "B "THERE
MAKE "C SENTENCE :A :B
PRINT :C
PRINT FIRST :C
```

LAST is similar to FIRST, except it returns the last item in a string, list, sentence, or word. Here is an example:

```
MAKE "A "HELLO
MAKE "B "THERE
MAKE "C SENTENCE :A :B
MAKE "D LAST :C
PRINT :C
PRINT :D
```

BUTFIRST and BUTLAST

BUTFIRST and BUTLAST are the complements of FIRST and LAST. They return the whole string without the first or last item. For example,

```
MAKE "A [THE QUICK YELLOW CANARY]
MAKE "B BUTFIRST :A
MAKE "C BUTLAST :A
PRINT :A
PRINT :B
PRINT :C
END
```

These functions are very useful for data-intensive programs. Information can be stored as long words or sentences and then read out again one item at a time by using FIRST, LAST, BUTFIRST, and BUTLAST. Here, for example, is a program that contains a list of data that is stored in a single variable. The program allows you to read the items one at a time simply by pressing any key on the keyboard.

```
; ***** READ DATA ROUTINE *****
;
;PRINT THE OPENING MESSAGE
PRINT "
PRINT [THIS ROUTINE PRINTS]
PRINT [A DATA LIST THAT HAS]
PRINT [BEEN STORED IN A STRING.]
PRINT [TO READ THE LIST, ONE]
PRINT [ITEM AT A TIME,]
;
LABEL "STARTOVER ; THIS STARTS THE ROUTINE (AGAIN)
PRINT [PRESS ANY KEY...]
PRINT "
;
;THE DATA IS STORED IN VARIABLE :A
MAKE "A [ITEM_ONE ITEM_TWO ITEM_THREE ITEM_FOUR XX]
;
;PUT A TEMPORARY COPY OF THE DATA IN VARIABLE :C
MAKE "C :A
;
;READ DATA ROUTINE
LABEL "READ DATA
MAKE "Q READCHAR
IF FIRST :C = "XX [GO "EOF]
PRINT FIRST :C
MAKE "C BUTFIRST :C
GO "READ DATA
;
LABEL "EOF ; END OF FILE MESSAGE
PRINT "
PRINT [THAT'S THE WHOLE LIST]
PRINT [DO YOU WANT TO READ]
PRINT [IT AGAIN? (Y / N)]
;
LABEL "YORN ; YES OR NO
MAKE "Q READCHAR
IF (AND (:Q <> "Y) (:Q <> "N)) [GO "RETRY]
IF :Q = "N [GO "FINISHED]
PRINT "Y
PRINT "
PRINT [OK, STARTING OVER...]
PRINT "
GO "STARTOVER
;
LABEL "RETRY
```

```
PRINT "
PRINT [PLEASE ENTER Y OR N.]
PRINT "
GO "YORN
;
LABEL "FINISHED
PRINT "N
PRINT "
PRINT [OK, ENDING...]
PRINT "
END
```

Take a look at what this program does and how it works. First, enter the program exactly as shown. (In the previous chapters, we showed the question mark prompt (?) and greater-than prompt (>) that the ST displays. For the sake of simplicity, from this point on the prompts are not shown; only the actual programs.)

In the first line the procedure is named DATA. The next nine lines display the opening message that describes the program and how it works. Remember: any text that appears to the right of a semicolon (;) is a remark and is ignored by the ST.

Notice that the last line of the opening message (PRESS ANY KEY...) is actually a part of the STARTOVER routine. This has been done because you want to provide the last part of the message every time you repeat the routine.

The next line puts data into the variable :A. Notice that the items are attached to the numbers by an underscore character (_). This is done to make the two words connect and still have a visible separation. As this routine is written, the items are read one at a time. You could have two items at a time read and printed together. In fact, you could have each letter read one at a time as well. For each letter to be read, the data would need to be listed as one continuous data string. In this case, however, you want the data read as whole words.

Next, you put a temporary, expendable copy of the data into a second variable, called :C, because you don't want to modify the data in variable :A. To read the individual words, first read a word and then remove it from the list. By creating a second copy of the data, you can remove words and then simply restore the list by copying the original.

The first thing the READ DATA routine does is read a character from the keyboard. Notice that the program assigns the value to the variable :Q. You could have assigned it to any variable, since the data isn't used (the program doesn't care which character was pressed). You need to assign the value, however, or the ST will not know what to do with the data it just read and will display this error message.

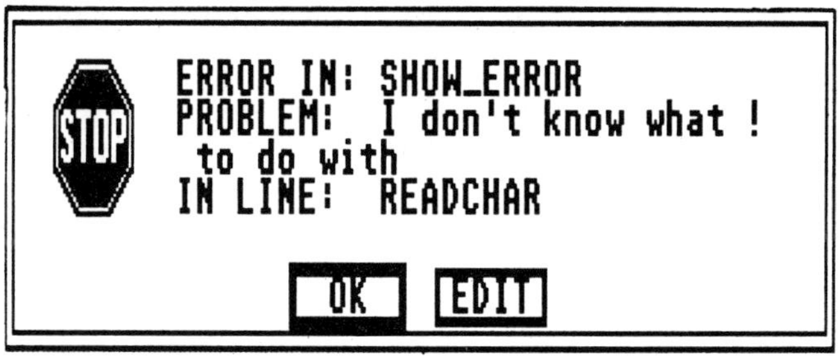

Take a look at the data again:

```
MAKE "A [ITEM_ONE ITEM_TWO ITEM_THREE ITEM_FOUR XX]
```

Notice that the last item listed is XX. This is *dummy data*. The computer doesn't use this data—it's simply an end-of-file marker. In the line after READCHAR, look at the data remaining in :C. If the only item left in :C is XX, then you know that you have read all of the valid data. The program branches to the label "EOF, which asks if you want to read the list again.

On the other hand, if the next item is not XX, the procedure prints the item, removes it from the list with the BUTFIRST command, and branches back to the label READ DATA.

The rest of the procedure is easy to use and understand. Designing a procedure's "user interface" will be discussed next.

INPUT AND OUTPUT PROGRAMMING

It is easy for beginning programmers to become acquainted with how LOGO calculates numbers. But as you can see from the previous program, when you write programs that receive input from the keyboard and display data on the screen, the programming becomes more tricky.

Nearly every program requires some kind of input from the keyboard. If you are the person operating the computer, you can probably put together some input statements that get the required data and process it in your program. But if someone else is operating the computer, sooner or later the wrong key will be pressed or an incorrect entry will be made. Every computer operator will make mistakes at some time. You should write programs that take this into account and allow for human error.

The same is true for output programming. If you display the results of a program with a set of PRINT statements, those results have to be readable to the person looking at the display. This does not happen by hacking away at program statements until the output looks a little better; you must give it some thought while you are writing the program.

Assume that you want to write a program that inputs names and addresses. You could write the program quickly and easily.

```
;***** NAME/ADDRESS PROCEDURE *****
;
;INTIALIZE VARIABLES
;
MAKE "NAME "
MAKE "STREET "
MAKE "CITY "
MAKE "STATE"
MAKE "ZIP "
MAKE "PHONE "
;
MAKE "X 1
LABEL "LOOP
TYPE [ENTER NAME] TYPE CHAR 32 PRINT :X
MAKE "NAME SENTENCE :NAME READQUOTE
TYPE [ENTER STREET ADDRESS] TYPE CHAR 32 PRINT :X
MAKE "STREET SENTENCE :STREET READQUOTE
TYPE [ENTER CITY] TYPE CHAR 32 PRINT :X
MAKE "CITY SENTENCE :CITY READQUOTE
TYPE [ENTER STATE] TYPE CHAR 32 PRINT :X
MAKE "STATE SENTENCE :STATE READQUOTE
TYPE [ENTER ZIP CODE] TYPE CHAR 32 PRINT :X
MAKE "ZIP SENTENCE :ZIP READQUOTE
TYPE [ENTER PHONE NUMBER] TYPE CHAR 32 PRINT :X
MAKE "PHONE SENTENCE :PHONE READQUOTE
MAKE "X :X + 1
IF :X = 21 [GO "FINISH]
GO "LOOP
LABEL "FINISH
END
```

Here is an example of how the program would appear on the display.

```
ENTER NAME 1
John Doe
ENTER STREET ADDRESS 1
1234 Street Place
ENTER CITY 1
Onion City
ENTER STATE 1
MN
ENTER ZIP CODE 1
12345
```

```
ENTER PHONE NUMBER 1
(000) 555-2468
ENTER NAME 2
Hugo Four
ENTER STREET ADDRESS 2
4123-B Never-Land Road
ENTER CITY 2
Whereville
ENTER STATE 2
NY
ENTER ZIP CODE 2
```

While running this program, the person entering names and addresses might discover a mistake in a name after pressing RETURN. But the operator can't go back to fix the name when the program is asking for address input.

Other problems with this program are obvious if you enter and run it. The display is not very easy to read—one entry for a name and address follows another, all the way down the screen. This kind of clutter will increase the possibility of incorrect entries.

Creating a Formatted Display

To allow for wider entries, it is usually best to set up the computer for medium- or high-screen resolution. If you have a monochrome (black-and-white) monitor, the ST will automatically be set up in high resolution. If you have a color monitor, you should select medium resolution. This must be done from the opening desktop. If you are currently set up in low resolution, go back to the desktop (by quitting LOGO).

From the desktop, select Set Preferences from the Options menu.

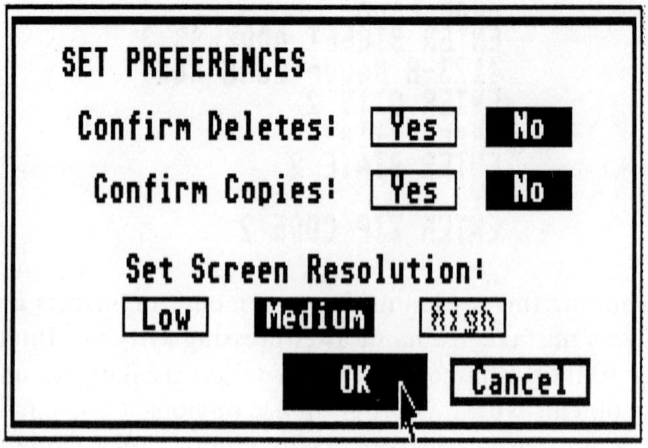

Simply click on the Medium box and then on the OK box. It is also a good idea to save the desktop at this point; then you won't have to change the resolution each time you start up. Now restart LOGO.

Formatted displays should be used in programs that require a good deal of data entry. Three distinguishing features of proper data entry techniques are an uncluttered display, clear directions to the operator, and the ability of the operator to correct mistakes.

Positioning Text: A First Look At the Graphics Display Window

Up to this point, all of the text that you have entered and displayed has appeared in the LOGO Dialog window. With simple programs that print one message after another, this is no problem. With programs that require data entry or some other kind of formatted display, however, it is difficult to work with the LOGO Dialog window, because everything prints strictly from top to bottom. In the Graphics Display window, we can put characters anywhere at all.

INTRODUCING THE TURTLE

When you look at the Graphics Display window, the first thing you notice is the small arrow in the center of the window. This is called the *turtle*. It is used to produce some of the graphics that LOGO can draw, and it is used as a pointer for text entries as well.

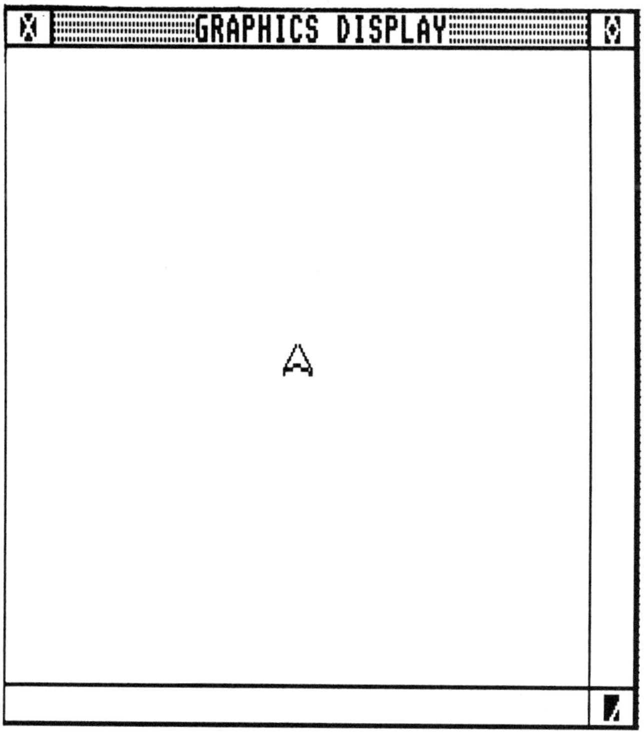

The turtle is a drawing tool. It is able to move and rotate within (and outside) the Graphics Display window. There are quite a few commands available to move the turtle. Perhaps the simplest is FORWARD. The FORWARD command simply tells the turtle to move a specified number of dots in the direction it is pointed. To understand how this works, enter the following:

```
FORWARD 50
```

Notice that the turtle moves up the screen about an inch and leaves a black trail behind it.

In high and medium resolution, the screen is divided into a maximum of 366 dots (sometimes called *pixels*) from top to bottom and 606 dots from right to left. However, the screen is actually 640×400 in high-resolution mode and 640×200 in medium-resolution mode. To compensate for the missing horizontal dots, medium-resolution mode only moves the turtle every other vertical dot. Horizontal dots are still acted upon one-for-one. To see this in action, enter the following (and press RETURN at the end of each line):

```
?FORWARD 1
?FORWARD 1
?FORWARD 1
?FORWARD 1
?FORWARD 1
?FORWARD 1
?FORWARD 1
?FORWARD 1
```

This way, the turtle moves roughly the same distance in both high-resolution and medium-resolution modes. This is because a single vertical forward movement in medium-resolution mode moves the turtle two dots up (or down) on every even-numbered dot, while every forward movement moves the turtle one dot up (or down).

In low-resolution mode, the ST's screen is 320×200 dots. Everything is four times as big as it is in high-resolution mode, and the turtle moves one dot for every forward command. For the moment, let's stick with medium- and high-resolution modes, since they are very similar in operation.

TURTLE TEXT

The TURTLETEXT primitive (abbreviated TT) tells LOGO to print some text on the Graphics Display window. For example, here is a routine that prints some text in the LOGO Dialog window and in the Graphics Display window.

```
CLEARSCREEN
;
;THIS WILL PRINT IN THE DIALOG WINDOW
PRINT [DIALOG WINDOW TEXT]
;
;THIS WILL PRINT IN THE GRAPHICS DISPLAY
TURTLETEXT [TURTLE TEXT]
```

Here is the graphics display created by the last line of the listing:

Notice that the text begins right on top of the turtle and prints to the right. When you use turtle text, the text will always begin directly to the right of the turtle.

If the text always begins on top of the turtle, the first letter will always be partially obliterated. To prevent this, you can make the turtle invisible using the HIDETURTLE primitive (abbreviated HT). Try this:

```
CLEARSCREEN
;
;THIS WILL MAKE THE TURTLE INVISIBLE
HIDETURTLE
;
;THIS WILL PRINT IN THE DIALOG WINDOW
PRINT [DIALOG WINDOW TEXT]
;
;THIS WILL PRINT IN THE GRAPHICS DISPLAY
TURTLETEXT [TURTLE TEXT]
```

The screen will look like this:

TURTLE TEXT

To make the turtle visible again, use the SHOWTURTLE primitive (ST). Whether the turtle is visible or not, its movements are still the same and they produce the same results on the screen. Thus, to print a line of text in the upper-left corner of the Graphics Display window, you'll need to move the turtle to the upper-left corner of the window (actually twelve dots down from the top of the window, since the turtle defines the lower-left corner of the first character).

RIGHT, LEFT, AND BACK

So far, you only know how to move the turtle forward. If this were the only direction, you would have a severely limited turtle. Fortunately, you can also move it backward (with the BACK command, abbreviated BK). In addition, you can rotate the turtle either clockwise (with the RIGHT command, abbreviated RT) or counterclockwise (with the LEFT command, abbreviated LT).

Using these new commands, enter the following line to move the turtle to the upper-left corner of the Graphics Display window. You should clear the screen before you put anything else on it. To do this, use the CLEARSCREEN command (CS). Try the following:

```
CLEARSCREEN
SHOWTURTLE
FORWARD 157
LEFT 90
FORWARD 138
RIGHT 90
```

The screen will look like this:

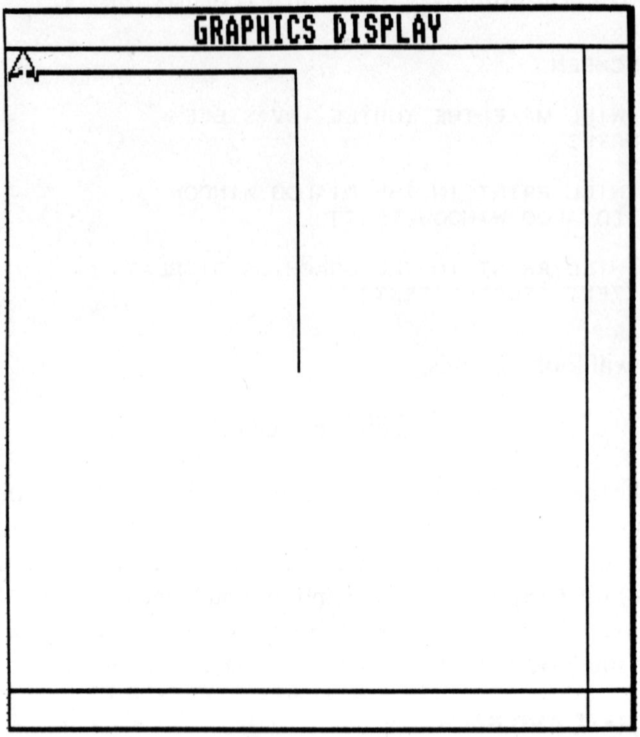

As you can see, this moved the turtle to the right spot in the window, but it also drew a couple of lines from the center of the window to the corner. To avoid this, use the PENUP primitive. Normally, the turtle will draw a line wherever it goes, using its imaginary "pen." To prevent this, use the PENUP (PU) command. To make the turtle draw again, use the PENDOWN (PD) command.

Position the turtle again, using PENUP before you move.

```
CLEARSCREEN
SHOWTURTLE
PENUP
FORWARD 157
```

```
LEFT 90
FORWARD 138
RIGHT 90
```

The Graphics Display window will look like this:

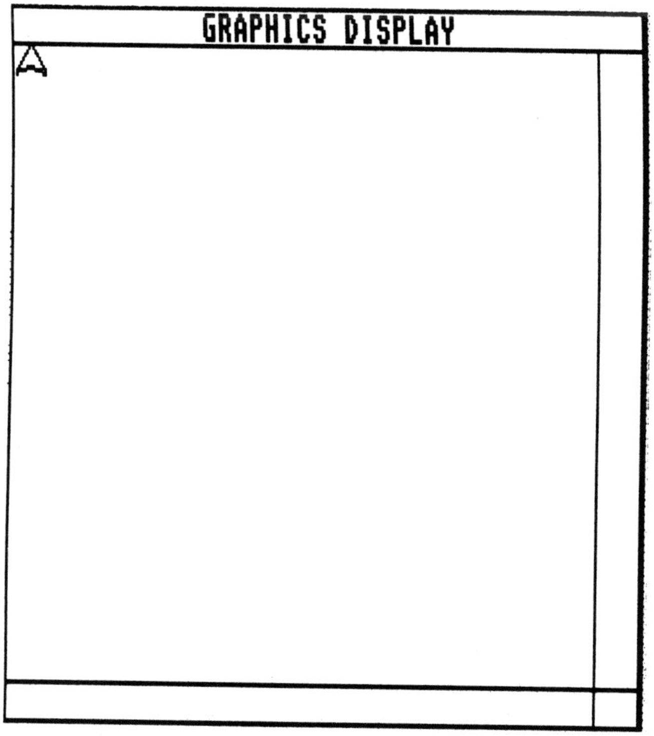

As you can see, the turtle did not draw a line this time — it simply entered the text into the upper-left corner of the window. Using this method, you can position text anywhere in the Graphics Display window. To postion text accurately, however, you will need to look at the actual character positions. Remember, the turtle positions are dot positions, not character positions.

In medium-resolution and high-resolution modes, the characters are 8 dots wide and 16 dots high. The window (if it is full-size) is 366 dots high and 606 dots wide. This means that you can display 22 rows with 75 characters in each row, which will produce a character grid as shown in Figure 4-1.

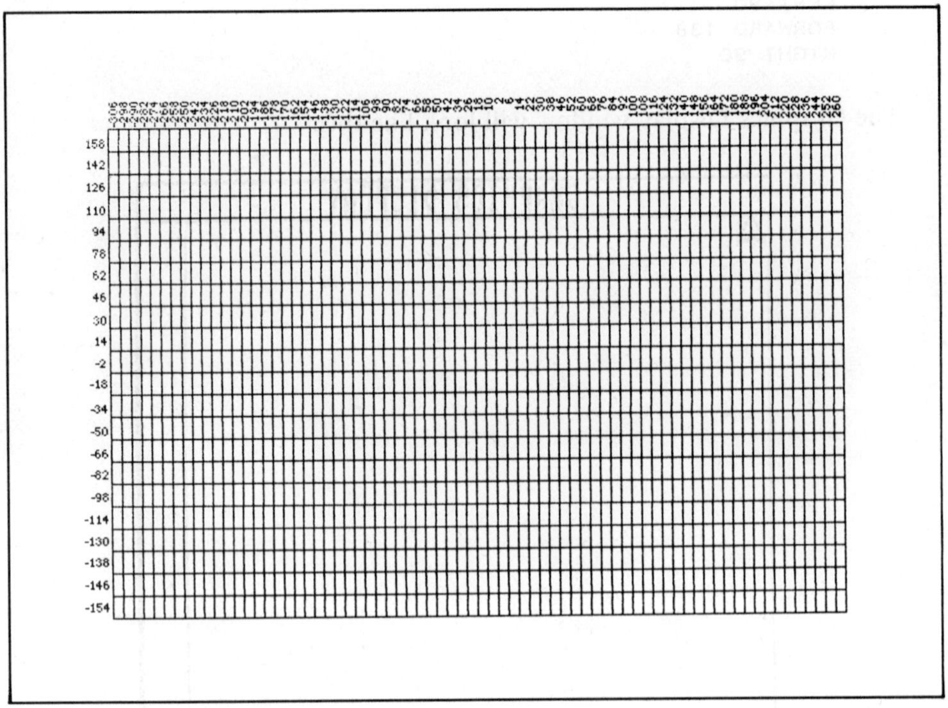

FIGURE 4-1. Logo character grid

A Cursor Movement Subprocedure

There is another command that you can use to position the turtle in the window: SETPOS. SETPOS moves the turtle to an absolute position in the window, retaining the turtle's direction.

By using the PU, PD, and SETPOS commands, it is possible to move to any coordinate position in the Graphics Display. In LOGO, the *home* position is the very center of the screen (0,0). On a typical text screen, home is the upper-left character position in the window. The next few examples will refer to the upper-left character position as home.

Since the center of the window is (0,0) for LOGO, you need to use both positive and negative coordinates if you want to position the characters anywhere in the window. If you were to use only positive coordinates, you would only be able to use the upper-right portion of the window.

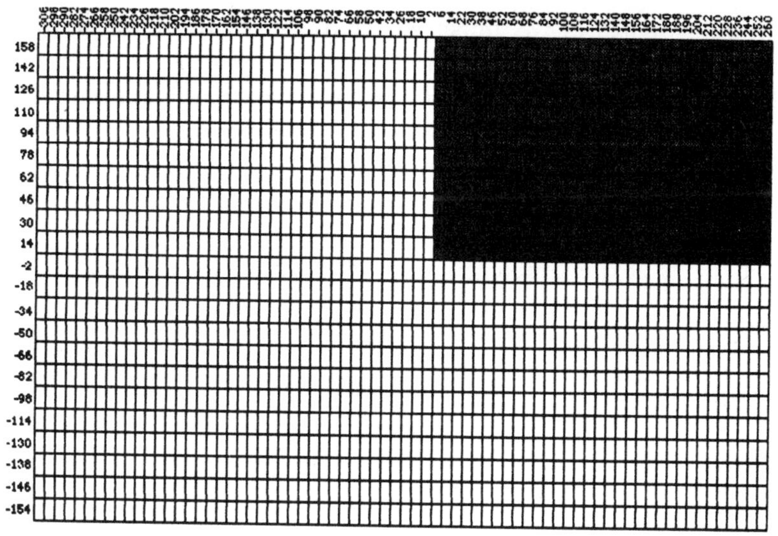

To move to the other three quadrants, you'll need to use negative coordinates. For example, in the upper-left quadrant the X (horizontal) coordinates must be negative and the Y (vertical) coordinates must be positive.

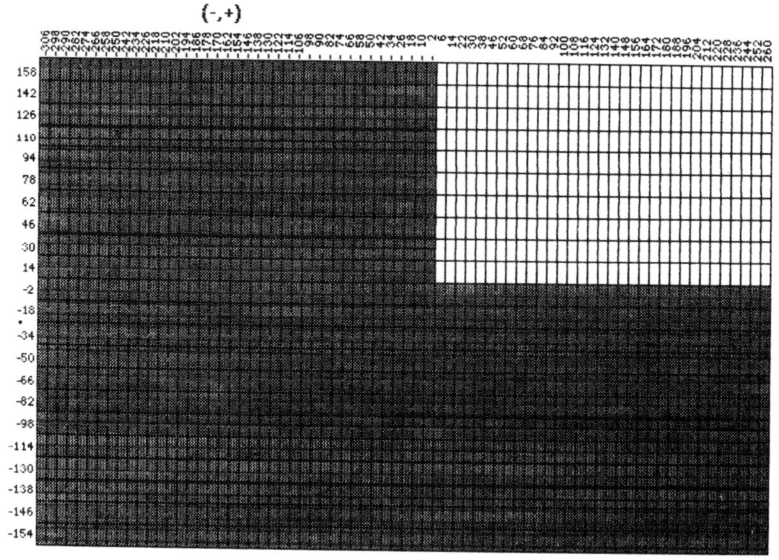

The coordinates of the upper-left character of the window will vary, depending upon the window's size and shape, but here are two sizes you will probably use most often. When LOGO first comes up, the Graphics Display window is half the size of the full screen, and the upper-left character position is (−149,158). In full-screen mode (after clicking in the Graphic Display window's Full box), the upper-left corner character will be (−306,158). You can move the cursor from this position to anywhere else in the window by calculating your next character position using the following procedure:

```
MAKE "R -306 + :ROW * 8
MAKE "C 158 - :COL * 16
MAKE "I SENTENCE :R :C
PU SETPOS :I PD
TT :CHR
```

As an example, here is a procedure that uses the POSITION subprocedure to type text in the Graphics Display window. In this example, two new operations are shown. First, you want to create a dummy display in the Graphics Display window. To do this, click on Graphics Display window's Full box (in its upper-right corner). Then select Save Pic... from the File menu. After you have created a dummy picture, you can open the window to full size (or any other size and shape you pre-save in a picture file) just by entering a command such as

LOADPIC "DUMMY

where DUMMY is the name of the blank screen. This procedure first opens the window and then continues with the text processing.

Next, you call a subprocedure named POSITION to put the characters in the window in their proper locations. You create a subprocedure, instead of using a LABEL as before, so that you can use this subprocedure in other procedures later in the book.

```
TO POSITION :ROW :COL :CHR
MAKE "R -306 + :ROW * 8
MAKE "C 158 - :COL * 16
MAKE "I SENTENCE :R :C
PU SETPOS :I PD
TT :CHR
END

TO TEXT_DISPLAY
LOADPIC "DUMMY
CS HT
MAKE "X 0
MAKE "Y 0
LABEL "NEXCHR
MAKE "Q READCHAR
```

```
POSITION :X :Y :Q
MAKE "X :X + 1
IF :X = 76 [GO "ADDY]
GO "NEXCHR
LABEL "ADDY
MAKE "X 0
MAKE "Y :Y + 1
GO "NEXCHR
END
```

The first line clears the screen, removing old text from the display (this has nothing to do with cursor positioning; it is just "housekeeping" to make a cleaner display). The variables ROW and COL in the procedure name refer to the horizontal and vertical character positions, and the variable CHR contains the character you want to print.

This cursor-movement subprocedure will be an integral part of creating and using formatted displays.

The CHAR Function: Programming Characters in ASCII

If you cannot press a key to include a character within a text string, you can still select the character by using its ASCII value.

The CHAR function translates an ASCII code number into its character equivalent. To obtain the ASCII code for a character, refer to Appendix A. Scan the columns until you find the desired character, and then note the corresponding ASCII code number. Insert this number right after the CHAR function. For example, to create the symbol $ from its ASCII code, look up the ASCII code for $ in Appendix A. The ASCII value for $ is 36. Insert 36 into the CHAR function as follows:

```
?PRINT CHAR 36
$
```

CHAR's opposite function is the ASCII function. It produces the ASCII (numeric) value of a character. Here is a short procedure that prints the ASCII and CHAR values of any character you type at the keyboard:

```
PRINT "
LABEL "LOOP
PRINT [ASCII CHAR]
MAKE "A READCHAR
TYPE CHAR 32
TYPE ASCII :A
REPEAT 5 [TYPE CHAR 32]
PRINT :A
GO "LOOP
END
```

The values will appear on the screen like this:

```
ASCII CHAR
 64     @
ASCII CHAR
 65     A
ASCII CHAR
 66     B
ASCII CHAR
 98     b
ASCII CHAR
 67     C
```

The CHAR function lets you include otherwise unavailable characters, such as the copyright symbol and the musical note symbol, in a TYPE statement's parameters.

You can also use the CHAR function to check for special characters like RETURN. Suppose a program must check character input at the keyboard, looking for a RETURN key. You could check for a RETURN (which has an ASCII code of 13) in this manner:

```
PRINT "
LABEL "LOOP
PRINT [ASCII CHAR]
MAKE "A READCHAR
IF :A = CHAR 13 [GO "LOOPOUT]
TYPE CHAR 32
TYPE ASCII :A
REPEAT 5 [TYPE CHAR 32]
PRINT :A
GO "LOOP
LABEL "LOOPOUT
TYPE CHAR 32
TYPE ASCII :A
REPEAT 3 [TYPE CHAR 32]
PRINT "RETURN
GO "LOOP
```

This test would be impossible if you tried to enter a RETURN after a quotation mark or inside brackets, because pressing the RETURN key automatically moves the cursor to the next line.

Data Entry (Input)

It is bad programming practice to break data input into its smallest parts. In a mailing-list program, for example, it would be bad programming practice to ask just for the name, process this data as soon as it is entered, and then ask for each line of the address, treating each piece of the name and address as a separate functional unit. This approach makes programs difficult to change and also renders them less readable. The goal of any data entry program should be to make it easy for an operator to spot errors and to give the operator as many chances as possible to fix them.

Data entry should be programmed in functional units. A good mailing-list program, for example, requires that names and addresses be entered as data. You should treat each entire name and address as a single functional unit rather than as separate data items. In other words, your program should ask for the name and address, allowing the operator to enter all of this information and then change any part of it. When the operator is satisfied that the name and address is correct, the program should process the entire name and address. The program should then ask for the next name and address.

Prompting Messages

Any program that requires data entry should prompt the operator by asking questions. Questions are usually displayed on a single line and require a simple response like "yes" or "no." For example, a prompt message such as ANY CHANGES (Y OR N)? would clearly indicate the question and the available choices.

An operator responds to this message by pressing the Y or N key. Good programming practice dictates that entries other than Y or N would not be accepted. If the operator replies Y to the ANY CHANGES prompt, another prompt such as WHAT ENTRY LINE TO CHANGE (1-6)? will display. In this case, one of six entry lines could be changed; the operator only needs to enter the number corresponding to the line that was entered in error. Of course, with this approach each entry line on the display should have an identifying number.

This type of data entry should be written in subprocedures, so that the main program will not be clogged up with prompting messages. Also, because a limited number of choices is allowed, a subprocedure should contain the logic necessary to check the entry against permitted responses.

This has two implications. First, the subprocedure must receive parameters from the calling program. For example, if a message asks the operator to enter a number, the calling program should pass the minimum and maximum allowed numbers to the subprocedure as parameters. Second, the subprocedure must return the operator's response to the calling program. This variable may be a character, a word, or a number.

A subprocedure that prompts for a reply of Y or N may use a PRINT statement to ask the question, followed by a READCHAR to receive a one-character response. Since you may have many questions that require a response of Y or N in a program, the subprocedure should also allow a prompt to be passed to the subprocedure from the main program in a variable. Here are the necessary statements:

```
;ASK A QUESTION AND RETURN A RESPONSE OF Y OR N IN YN
PRINT [DO YOU WANT TO MAKE ANY CHANGES?]
PRINT [Y OR N]
LABEL "GETCHR
MAKE "YN READCHAR
IF AND (:YN <> "Y) (:YN <> "N) [GO "RET]
PRINT :YN
GO "FINISH
LABEL "RET
PRINT [PLEASE ENTER Y OR N]
GO "GETCHR
LABEL "FINISH
```

In this example the printed prompt DO YOU WANT TO MAKE ANY CHANGES? could be replaced with a variable like QU if you wanted the routine to ask different questions at different times in your procedure. If you did this, the variable QU would have to be set in the program that calls the subprocedure. The subprocedure is generalized—that is, it displays any prompt sent to it by the main program. The response is returned to the main program in the string variable YN.

Now consider dialogue that allows an operator to enter a number. Assume that the main program passes to the subprocedure the lowest allowable numeric entry as LO and the highest as HI. Once the operator enters a number within range, the subprocedure will return the entered number in NM. Here is the subprocedure that gets the keyboard entry, checks it against LO and HI values, and then passes it back to the main program in NM:

```
;ASK FOR A NUMERIC SELECTION
;RETURN THE NUMBER IN :NM
;NM MUST BE <= :HI AND >= :LO
TYPE :QU TYPE CHAR 32
LABEL "GETCHR
MAKE "NM READCHAR
IF OR (:NM < :LO) (:NM > :HI) [GO "GETCHR]
PRINT :NM
```

Write a short program that sets values for HI and LO and then goes to the subprocedure. Add the previous subprocedure and run it.

Can you change the subprocedure so that it accepts two-digit input? Try to write this modified program for yourself.

Entering a Valid Date

Most programs need relatively simple data input — more than a simple yes or no, but less than a full-screen display. A good example of this is a date.

You must be careful with such apparently simple data entry. In all likelihood, the date will be just one item in a data-entry sequence. By carefully designing data entry for each small item, you can avoid having to restart a long data-entry sequence whenever the operator makes a mistake in a single entry.

Assume the date is to be entered as follows:

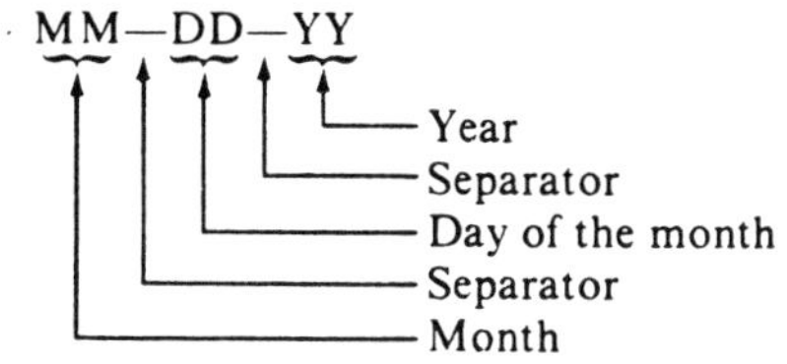

The dashes that separate the month, day, and year could be slashes or any other appropriate characters.

You should program data entry so that it is pleasing to the operator's eye. The operator should be able to see immediately where data is to be entered, what type of data is required, and how far data entry has proceeded. A good way of showing where the data is to be entered is to display the entry line in inverse video or in a contrasting color. For example, the program that asks for a date might create the following display:

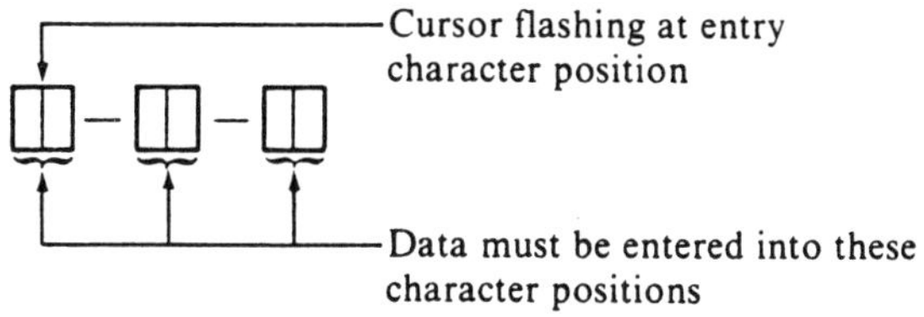

You can create such a display with the following statement:

```
TO POSITION :ROW :COL :CHR
MAKE "R -149 + :ROW * 8
MAKE "C 158 - :COL * 16
MAKE "I SENTENCE :R :C
PU SETPOS :I PD
TT :CHR
END
```

```
TO DATE_FORM
CS HT
MAKE "X 10
MAKE "Y 10
MAKE "FORM [__ - __ - __]
POSITION :X :Y :FORM
MAKE "X 10
MAKE "Y 11
MAKE "FORM [MM - DD - YY]
POSITION :X :Y :FORM
END
```

The PRINT statement in this example positions the date entry beginning at column 6 in row 3. The PRINT statement also clears the screen so that no residual display surrounds the request for a date. After displaying the data entry line, the PRINT statement moves the cursor back to the first position of the entry line by using the SETPOS and TT commands.

Try using a READCHAR statement to receive the entry for month. This can be done as follows:

```
MAKE "ZZ READCHAR
POSITION :X :Y :ZZ
MAKE "X :X + 1
MAKE "YY READCHAR
POSITION :X :Y :YY
MAKE "M WORD :ZZ :YY
```

These statements accept the entire month, day, and year as separate characters. They are then combined into the three parts of the date. The date input needs no RETURN or other terminating character. The program automatically terminates the data entry after the entire date has been entered.

```
TO POSITION :ROW :COL :CHR
MAKE "R -148 + :ROW * 8
MAKE "C 158 - :COL * 16
MAKE "I SENTENCE :R :C
PU SETPOS :I PD PX
TT :CHR
END

TO MAKEFORM
CS HT
MAKE "X 10
MAKE "Y 11
MAKE "FORM [MM - DD - YY]
POSITION :X :Y :FORM
MAKE "X 10
MAKE "Y 10
MAKE "FORM [__ - __ - __]
POSITION :X :Y :FORM
END
```

```
TO GETDATPR :QQ
POSITION :X :Y "_
POSITION :X :Y "=
MAKE "ZZ READCHAR
IF :ZZ = CHAR 13 [FIG_4_2]
POSITION :X :Y "=
POSITION :X :Y :ZZ
MAKE "X :X + 1
POSITION :X :Y "_
POSITION :X :Y "=
MAKE "JJ READCHAR
POSITION :X :Y "=
POSITION :X :Y :JJ
IF :JJ = CHAR 13 [FIG_4_2]
MAKE :QQ WORD :ZZ :JJ
MAKE "X :X + 4
END

TO DATE_FORM
MAKEFORM
GETDATPR "M
GETDATPR "D
GETDATPR "Y
END
```

The variables M, D, and Y hold the month, day, and year entries, respectively. Each entry is held as a two-character string.

There are two ways to help the operator recover from errors while entering a date. The program can automatically test for valid month, day, and year entries, or the operator can restart data entry by pressing a specific key.

The program checks that the month lies between 01 and 12. It will not bother with leap years but will check for the maximum number of days in the specified month. Any year from 00 through 99 is allowed. Any invalid entry restarts the entire date entry sequence. Also, if the operator presses the RETURN key, the entire date-entry sequence restarts. The final date-entry program appears in Figure 4-2.

Three items are checked in the data as it is entered:

- Is the character a RETURN?
- If the character is not a RETURN, is it a valid digit?
- Is the two-character combination a valid month for the first entry, a valid day for the second entry, or a valid year for the third entry?

The RETURN has been selected as an abort (restart) character. By replacing CHAR 13 in the procedure, you can select any other abort character. When the operator presses the selected abort key, the entire date-entry sequence restarts. You must check for the abort character in the two-character

```
TO POSITION :ROW :COL :CHR
MAKE "R -148 + :ROW * 8
MAKE "C 158 - :COL * 16
MAKE "I SENTENCE :R :C
PU SETPOS :I PD PX
TT :CHR
END

TO MAKEFORM
CS HT
MAKE "X 10
MAKE "Y 11
MAKE "FORM [MM - DD - YY]
POSITION :X :Y :FORM
MAKE "X 10
MAKE "Y 10
MAKE "FORM [__ - __ - __]
POSITION :X :Y :FORM
END

TO GETDATPR :QQ
POSITION :X :Y "_
POSITION :X :Y "=
MAKE "ZZ READCHAR
IF :ZZ = CHAR 13 [FIG_4_2]
POSITION :X :Y "=
POSITION :X :Y :ZZ
MAKE "X :X + 1
POSITION :X :Y "_
POSITION :X :Y "=
MAKE "JJ READCHAR
POSITION :X :Y "=
POSITION :X :Y :JJ
IF :JJ = CHAR 13 [FIG_4_2]
MAKE :QQ WORD :ZZ :JJ
MAKE "X :X + 4
END

TO CHECKDATE
MAKE "MM 31
MAKE "M :M + 0
MAKE "D :D + 0
MAKE "Y :Y + 0
IF OR (:Y > 99) (:Y < 1) [BADATE]
IF OR (:M > 12) (:M < 1) [BADATE]
IF OR (:M = 4) (:M = 6) [MAKE "MM 30]
IF OR (:M = 9) (:M = 11) [MAKE "MM 30]
IF :M = 2 [MAKE "MM 28]
IF :D > :MM [BADATE]
END
```

FIGURE 4-2. A simple program for entering and verifying the data

```
TO BADATE
MAKE "X 10
MAKE "Y 14
MAKE "FORM [YOU HAVE ENTERED]
POSITION :X :Y :FORM
MAKE "X 10
MAKE "Y 15
MAKE "FORM [AN INVALID DATE]
POSITION :X :Y :FORM
MAKE "X 10
MAKE "Y 17
MAKE "FORM [PLEASE RE - ENTER DATE]
POSITION :X :Y :FORM
MAKE "X 10
MAKE "Y 14
MAKE "FORM [YOU HAVE ENTERED]
POSITION :X :Y :FORM
MAKE "X 10
MAKE "Y 15
MAKE "FORM [AN INVALID DATE]
POSITION :X :Y :FORM
MAKE "X 10
MAKE "Y 17
MAKE "FORM [PLEASE RE - ENTER DATE]
POSITION :X :Y :FORM
FIG_4_2
END

TO DATEOK
MAKE "X 10
MAKE "Y 13
MAKE "FORM [YOU HAVE ENTERED]
POSITION :X :Y :FORM
MAKE "X 10
MAKE "Y 14
MAKE "FORM [A VALID DATE]
POSITION :X :Y :FORM
END

TO ENTER_DATE
MAKEFORM
GETDATPR "M
GETDATPR "D
GETDATPR "Y
CHECKDATE
DATEOK
END
```

FIGURE 4-2. A simple program for entering and verifying the data (*continued*)

input subprocedure, since you may want to abort after the first or second digit has been entered.

The main program also checks for an abort character in order to branch back to the LOOP statement and restart the entire date-entry sequence. You could branch out of the two-character input subprocedure to the DATE statement in the calling program, thereby eliminating the abort-character test in the calling program, but this is not recommended. Every subprocedure should be treated as a module, with specified entry points and standard subprocedure return points.

Program logic that tests for characters that are not digits can reside entirely in the two-character input subprocedure. This program ignores nondigit characters. The subprocedure tests for nondigit characters by comparing the ASCII value of the input character and the ASCII values for the allowed numeric digits. The calling program must contain logic to check for valid month, day, and year, since each of these 2-character values has different allowed limits.

The subprocedure uses a numeric equivalent of the month, but not of the day or the year. This is because the day and year are not used very often, but the month is used in several lines. You will save both memory and execution time by using a numeric representation of the month.

It takes time to write a good data-entry program that checks for valid data input and allows the operator to restart at any time. By all means, the extra time is worthwhile. You will write a program once, while an operator may have to run the program many times. Thus, by spending extra programming time once, you may save operators many delays.

Formatted Data Input

The best way of handling multi-item data entry is to display a form and then fill it in as data is entered. Here is a formatted name-and-address display. You could have used this instead of the unformatted display earlier in this chapter.

```
ENTER NAME AND ADDRESS

1 NAME    ____________________
2 STREET  ____________________
3 CITY    ____________________
4 STATE   ____________________
5 ZIP     ____________________
6 PHONE   ____________________
```

Each entry line has a corresponding number. The form displays the number in inverse video. The operator enters data, starting with item 1 and ending with item 6. The operator can then change any specific data-entry line.

The following statements clear the screen and display the initial form:

```
TO POSITION :ROW :COL :CHR
MAKE "R -149 + :ROW * 8
MAKE "C 158 - :COL * 16
MAKE "I SENTENCE :R :C
PU SETPOS :I PD
TT :CHR
END

TO INVERTCHR
SETH 0 PU BK 1 PX
REPEAT 4 [FD 13 RT 90 FD 1 RT 90 FD 13 LT 90 FD 1 LT 90]
END

TO LINES
MAKE "X 4
MAKE "FORM [________________________]
REPEAT 6 [MAKE "X :X + 1 POSITION 12 :X :FORM]
END

TO PEELOFF :TEXT
MAKE "FORM SENTENCE ITEM 1 :TEXT ITEM 2 :TEXT
END

TO LISTING_4_27
CS HT
MAKE "FORM [ENTER NAME AND ADDRESS]
POSITION 3 3 :FORM
MAKE "TEXT [1 NAME 2 STREET 3 CITY 4 STATE 5 ZIP 6 PHONE]
MAKE "X 5
REPEAT 6 [PEELOFF :TEXT REPEAT 2 [MAKE "TEXT BF :TEXT] POSITION 3 :X :FORM INVE
RTCHR MAKE "X :X + 1]
LINES
END
```

RANDOM NUMBERS

Random numbers can be used in games you program on your 520-ST; they have more practical uses in statistics and other areas as well. The 520-ST will generate random numbers with the RANDOM function. RANDOM provides a real number between 32767 and −32768.

Generating Random Dice Throws

As an example using random numbers, here is a procedure that produces random dice throws. In it you generate two separate numbers in the range from 1 to 6.

```
TO THROW_DICE
HIDETURTLE
CLEARSCREEN
PENUP
SETPOS [-60 30]
```

```
DRAW_DICE
PENUP
SETPOS [30 30]
DRAW_DICE
ROLL
SHOW_ROLL
END

TO DRAW_DICE
PENDOWN
SETH 180
REPEAT 4 [FORWARD 30 LEFT 90]
SETH 46
FORWARD 10
SETH 90
FORWARD 30
RIGHT 90

FORWARD 30
RIGHT 45
FORWARD 10
SETH 0
FORWARD 30
RIGHT 45
FORWARD 10
END

TO ROLL
MAKE "A RANDOM 6
MAKE "B RANDOM 6
END

TO SHOW_ROLL
PENUP
SETPOS [-47 10]
PENDOWN
TURTLETEXT :A
PENUP
SETPOS [42 10]
PENDOWN
TURTLETEXT :B
END

TO T
THROW_DICE
END
```

Look at the subprocedure called T. The procedure is named THROW_DICE, because good programming practices indicate that procedures and programs should be clearly named. Unfortunately, this also makes it time-consuming to enter. The subprocedure has only one purpose—to run the procedure named THROW_DICE.

Random Selection of Playing Cards

The THROW_DICE procedure demonstrates an example in which the odds of getting the same results are always the same. There are some situations, however, in which the odds must be changed. For example, if you are dealing cards from a deck, each card can only be dealt once. The program below shows one way to program the shuffling of a deck of cards on the 520-ST. This program fills a 52-element table with the numbers 1 through 52 in a random sequence. The cards can be pegged to the random numbers in any way, such as

A = 1, 2 = 2, 3 = 3, ..., Q = 12, K = 13
Spades = 0, Hearts = 13, Diamonds = 26, Clubs = 42

With this scheme, the ace of spades=1+0=1, the queen of spades=12+0=12, the three of hearts=3+13=16, and so on. Note that element D (0) is not used.

In the shuffle program, a 52-element table called DISCARDS keeps track of whether a card has been chosen. PRINT statements are inserted to display the card number and value. Note that exactly 52 numbers are displayed and that no number is repeated. Each program run will produce a new random sequence.

```
TO DEAL_CARDS
MAKE "CNTR 1
MAKE "DISCARDS "0
LABEL "DRAW_CARD
MAKE "CARD RANDOM 52
MAKE "SPARE_DECK :DISCARDS
LABEL "CHECK_CARDS
IF :CARD = FIRST :SPARE_DECK [GO "DRAW_CARD]
IF COUNT :SPARE_DECK = 1 [GO "SELECT_CARD]
MAKE "SPARE_DECK BUTFIRST :SPARE_DECK
GO "CHECK_CARDS
LABEL "SELECT_CARD
TYPE :CNTR TYPE CHAR 9 PRINT :CARD
MAKE "CNTR :CNTR + 1
MAKE "DISCARDS SENTENCE :CARD :DISCARDS
GO "DRAW_CARD
END
```

Notice that this program runs more slowly as it nears the fifty-second number. It is especially slow on the last card. This occurs because the program has to fetch more and more random numbers to find one that has not already been picked. A simple routine like this has much room for improvement, of course. You can speed it up just by finding the last number in the program from the table, rather than waiting until it is selected randomly.

CHAPTER

Programming The Keyboard And the Mouse

5

The programs described so far have set up communications between you and the computer in a "stop-and-go" fashion; that is, they stopped and waited for you to type something at the keyboard and then acted on it. This is fine for balancing a checkbook or typing letters, but many 520-ST applications require a different style of communication. A program that simulated airplane flying wouldn't be realistic if the plane stopped in mid-air while the "pilot" typed instructions. To make this type of program more realistic (and less tedious to use), the ST takes its directions from a different source. Instead of receiving instructions through the keyboard, the ST receives them through the mouse.

This chapter will teach you to write programs that use the mouse. You'll also learn to use the keyboard "on the run," without the stop-and-wait steps.

USING THE MOUSE AS A CONTROLLER

The mouse controls up-and-down and side-to-side motion. It does so with a rolling ball and optical detectors. Figure 5-1 shows the wheels inside the mouse that spin as the mouse is moved. If the mouse is moved up and down only, or left and right only, just one wheel rotates, as shown in Figure 5-2. If the mouse is moved diagonally, two of the wheels rotate, as shown in Figure 5-3.

There are also two mouse buttons, each of which has its own switch. Using the method described in the following sections, your program can tell whether the button switches are open or closed and which wheels are moving (and in which direction). In this way the ST keeps track of the mouse position. By moving the mouse and reading its position, you can direct elements on the screen.

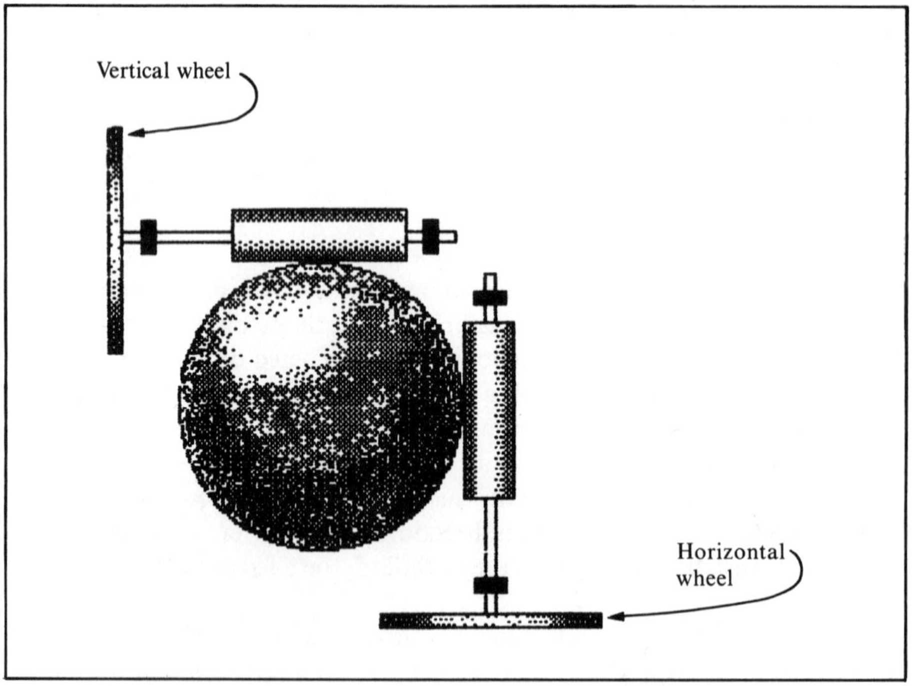

FIGURE 5-1. Inside the mouse

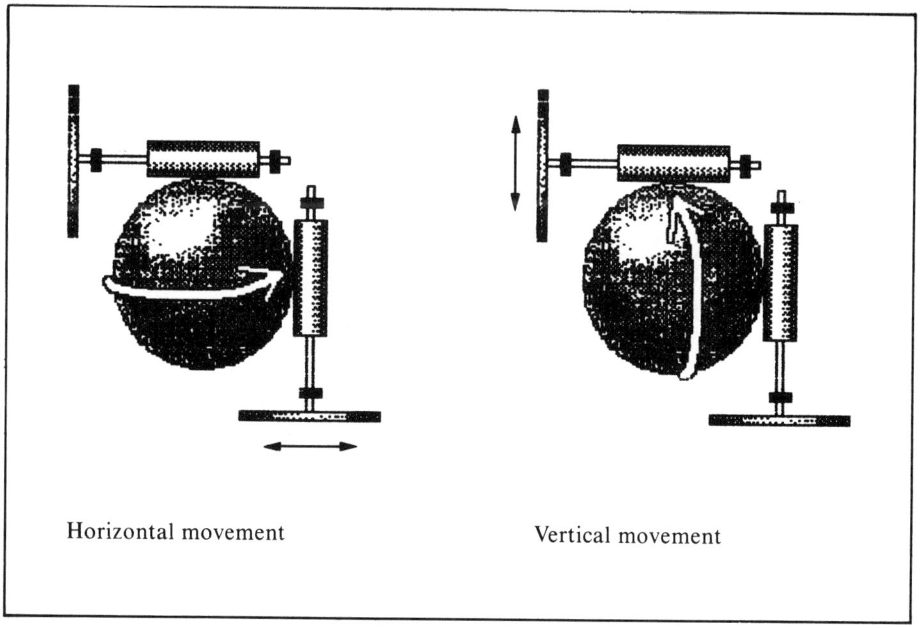

FIGURE 5-2. Horizontal and vertical movement

Reading the Mouse

The LOGO command that "reads" the mouse is called MOUSE. Position the mouse arrow so it is outside the Graphics Display window and type this command:

```
?MOUSE
```

The ST will respond with

[0 0 FALSE FALSE FALSE]

The first two numeric values indicate the mouse's position inside the Graphics Display window. When the mouse is outside the Graphics Display window, these values will always be (0,0). Try putting the mouse in the Graphics Display window and entering this command again.

The next two items report the status of the mouse buttons. The first of these reports on the left mouse button and the second reports on the right button. When the button is up (not pressed), this value is FALSE; when the button is down (pressed), the value is TRUE. The last item indicates where the

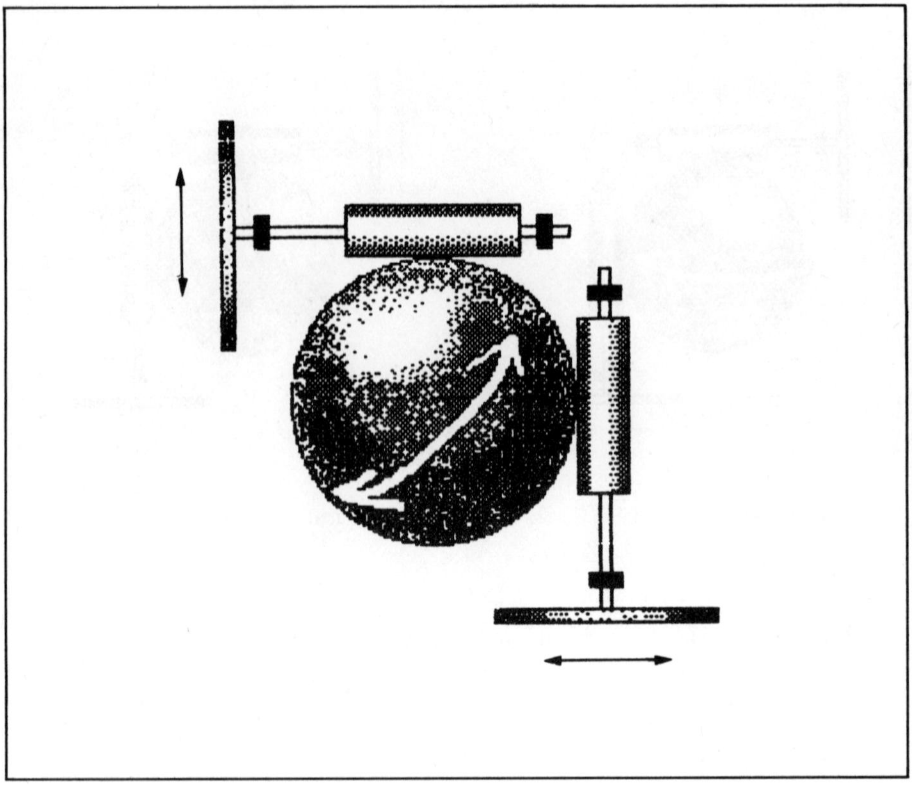

FIGURE 5-3. Diagonal movement

mouse is on the screen. If it is somewhere inside the Graphics Display window, this will be TRUE; if it is anywhere else, this will be FALSE.

Locating the Mouse

As you move the mouse around in the Graphics Display window, the values in the MOUSE command will follow the mouse. To get an idea of how this works, enter and run the following procedure:

```
TO READMOUSE
CLEARSCREEN
PENREVERSE
MAKE "B CHAR 32
LABEL "GETMOUSE
TURTLETEXT :B
```

```
MAKE "A PIECE 1 2 MOUSE
TURTLETEXT :A
MAKE "B :A
GO "GETMOUSE
END
```

One application for this is a drawing program. The following procedure draws a line that follows the mouse arrow in the Graphics Display window.

```
TO MOUSE_DRAW
CLEARSCREEN
HIDETURTLE
PENREVERSE
LABEL "DRAW
SETPOS MOUSE
GO "DRAW
END
```

Notice that this procedure is very speed-sensitive. This speed limitation is imposed by ST LOGO. You can, however, take advantage of LOGO's slow response time to produce straight lines.

Reading the Buttons

One disadvantage of the preceding procedure just given is that the mouse is always drawing; you cannot make it stop and start. A better routine would use the buttons to start and stop the drawing. In the following procedure, the mouse will only draw while the left mouse button is down:

```
TO MOUSE_DRAW
CLEARSCREEN
HIDETURTLE
PENREVERSE
LABEL "DRAW
IF ITEM 3 MOUSE = "FALSE [PU]
IF ITEM 3 MOUSE = "TRUE [PD]
SETPOS MOUSE
GO "DRAW
END
```

KEYBOARD COMMUNICATION USING THE READCHAR STATEMENT

In Chapter 3, you have seen the READCHAR and READQUOTE procedures. Those programs that use READQUOTE are the stop-and-go kind—if they need information from the keyboard, they have to wait for it. If you want to write an action program that receives instructions from the keyboard, you can use the READCHAR statement.

Like READQUOTE, the READCHAR statement reads information from the keyboard. The main differences between the two are as follows:

- READQUOTE reads one or more complete strings. READCHAR reads only a single keystroke.
- When you use READQUOTE, the program waits for you to press RETURN. If RETURN is not typed, your program will wait indefinitely. READCHAR, on the other hand, only expects a single character, not a RETURN.
- When you are typing in response to a READQUOTE, the characters you type appear on the screen. READCHAR doesn't echo what you type.

READCHAR Statement Syntax

The syntax of READCHAR is quite simple:

MAKE *variable name* READCHAR

No options are available. You must have exactly one variable. You can make a special prompt by using a PRINT or TYPE statement before the READCHAR statement.

```
TO PROMPT
PRINT [THIS IS A PROMPT, PRESS A KEY]
MAKE "A READCHAR
END
```

As mentioned earlier, characters entered with READCHAR do not appear on the screen. Sometimes, however, you need to see what you type. This can be accomplished by adding a PRINT statement to the program.

```
TO PROMPT
PRINT [THIS IS A PROMPT, PRESS A KEY]
MAKE "A READCHAR
PRINT :A
END
```

The Keyboard as Joystick

This section shows you how to create a "make-believe" joystick that will act like the ones made for video games. You can make the joystick point in various directions (left, right, up, down, and diagonally) by pressing different keys. It will also have a fire button, although it can't be pushed while a direction key is being held down.

Nine keys are needed for the joystick—eight for the various pointing directions and one for the fire button. The keys should be arranged so that they are easy to use. The following arrangement uses the keys that are naturally under your right hand when you are touch-typing. Their circular pattern is easy to learn and remember.

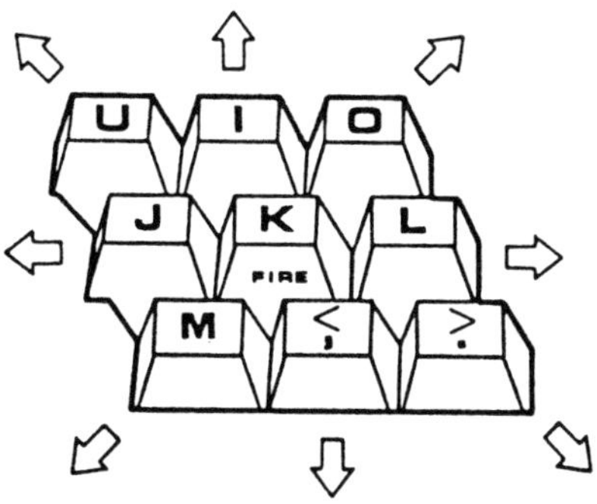

Now take a look at the programming necessary to interpret the keys and simulate the joystick. This routine creates labels that have the same names as the keys themselves. By doing this, the keys themselves call their routines. For example, pressing the U key will assign the letter I to the variable :A. The procedure then branches (using GO) to the label that corresponds to the value in :A—in this case, the UP routine labeled I.

```
TO JOY_KEY
; --- INITIALIZE SCREEN ---
CS HT PD
; --- READ "JOYSTICK" ---
LABEL "GETPOS
MAKE "A READCHAR
GO :A
; --- UP/LEFT ---
LABEL "U
SETH 315 FD 1
GO "GETPOS
; --- UP ---
LABEL "I
SETH 0 FD 1
GO "GETPOS
; --- UP/RIGHT ---
LABEL "O
SETH 45 FD 1
GO "GETPOS
```

```
; --- RIGHT ---
LABEL "L
SETH 90 FD 1
GO "GETPOS
; --- DOWN/RIGHT ---
LABEL ".
SETH 135 FD 1
GO "GETPOS
; --- DOWN ---
LABEL ",
SETH 180 FD 1
GO "GETPOS
; --- DOWN/LEFT ---
LABEL "M
SETH 225 FD 1
GO "GETPOS
; --- LEFT ---
LABEL "J
SETH 270 FD 1
GO "GETPOS
; --- FIRE BUTTON ---
LABEL "K
PX
TT "FIRE
REPEAT 10 [MAKE "A 1]
TT "FIRE
PD
GO "GETPOS
END
```

When you run this program, it looks at the keys you press and automatically converts the keystrokes into dot movements on the screen. Unfortunately, if you press a key that has not been defined (such as G), you'll get this message:

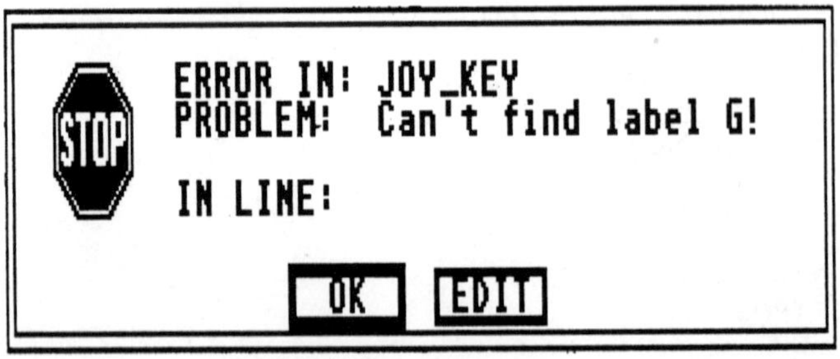

Of course it would be very time-consuming to write a routine that defines every possible keystroke. It would also make the program quite a bit slower. Fortunately, LOGO has a command that can capture errors and allow you to intercept the error messages. The command is CATCH.

The following procedure catches any errors that may occur in JOY_KEY and restarts the program when they occur.

```
TO RUN_JOY
CATCH "ERROR [JOY_KEY]
RUN RUN_JOY
RUN_JOY
END
```

CHAPTER

Graphics 6

In this book "graphics" means the display of pictures, rather than of text, data, or programs on the screen. The picture could be a face, an architectural drawing, a geometric shape, or simply an arrangement of text characters.

The 520-ST has extensive graphics capabilities. Some of these, such as the built-in graphics characters and the LOGO turtle, have been mentioned in the preceding chapters. These features will be explored in more detail in this chapter, and the ST's other graphics features, such as its ability to produce complex shapes with single commands, will be described as well. You will also learn programming techniques for using these features, which will help you to produce detailed and colorful displays.

Take another look at the Graphics Display window, our "canvas" for text and graphics artistry, which is shown in Figure 6-1. Notice the turtle in the center of the window. This is the positioning device that you will use to put most of the graphics shapes you produce into the window. The Graphics Display window is the graphics working area of the screen. Both the text and the graphics created by your programs in this chapter are displayed here.

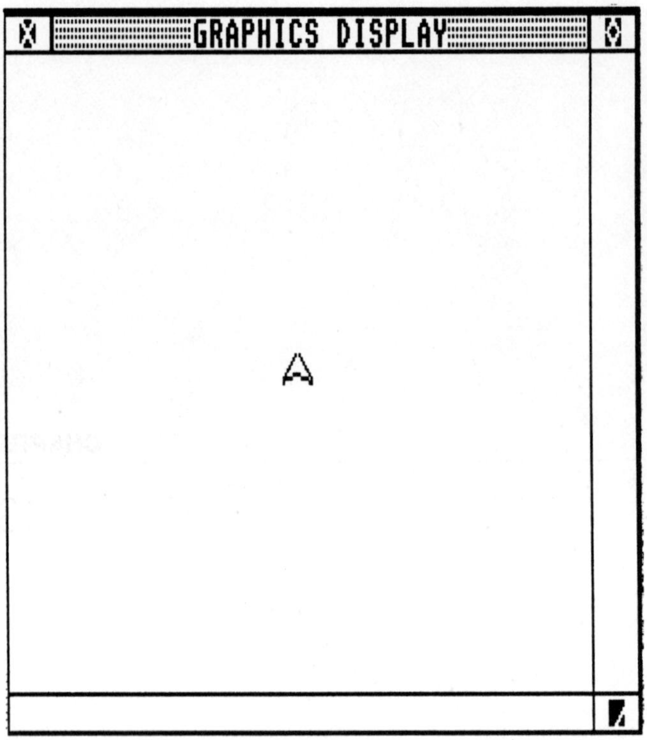

FIGURE 6-1. Graphics Display window

GRAPHICS MODES

The ST has two ways of creating graphics on the screen: by using the turtle and by using shape commands. In this first section you'll look at line drawings and at how the turtle moves around in the Graphics Display window.

Lines

In previous chapters, you used the flexibility of the Graphics Display window to enter and manipulate text. In this first graphics section, you will begin drawing. Your first tool is the turtle in the center of the Graphics Display window. If the turtle is not visible in your display (as it appears in Figure 6-1), enter **CS ST** and press RETURN. This is the abbreviation for CLEARSCREEN (CS) and SHOWTURTLE (ST). These commands will clear the display, return the turtle to the center of the window, and make it visible.

Now that the turtle is in its home position, enter the following to draw your first line:

```
?FORWARD 10
```

If you look closely at your screen, you will see that the line that follows the turtle originates at the rear edge of the turtle. If you make the turtle back up one dot, the line will actually be partially inside the turtle.

As you may recall, in addition to moving the turtle forward and backward, you can rotate the turtle into any position. The rotational positions are defined in degrees; 0 and 360 both mean straight up (the turtle's home direction).

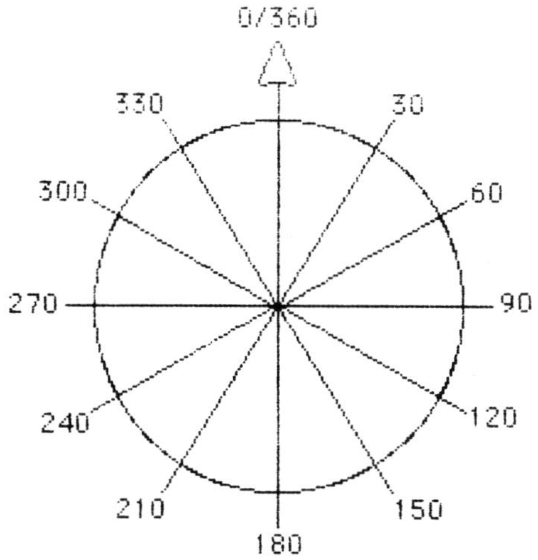

Here is a procedure that rotates the turtle through the full 360 degrees, drawing short lines every 6 degrees and longer lines every 30 degrees.

```
TO CLOCKFACE
CS HT
MAKE "A 0
FD 1 BK 2 FD 1
LABEL "INCR
MAKE "A :A + 6
SETH :A
IF :A / 30 = INT :A / 30 [GO "LONGLINE]
IF :A > 360 [GO "FIN]
GO "SHORTLINE
LABEL "SHORTLINE
```

```
PU FD 50 PD FD 5 PU BK 55 PD
GO "INCR
GO "LONGLINE
LABEL "LONGLINE
PU FD 40 PD FD 15 PU BK 55 PD
GO "INCR
LABEL "FIN
END
```

The result resembles a clock face.

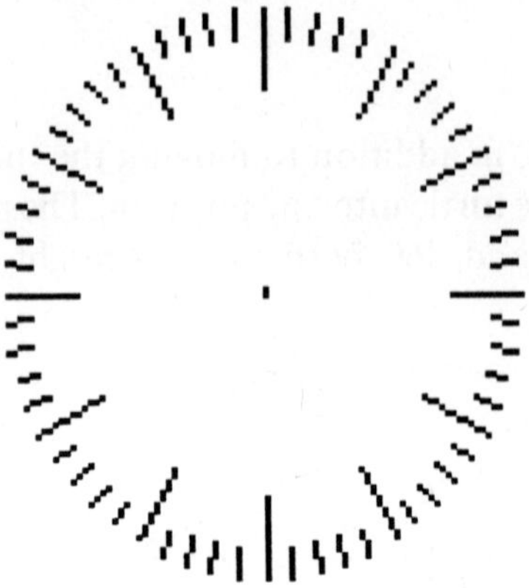

By positioning the turtle in the window, rotating it, and moving it around, you can draw almost any shape. Here is a procedure that accepts a number as input. The number represents the number of sides of the shape that will be drawn. For example, entering 3 will produce a triangle, while 5 will produce a pentagon. Try entering this procedure and see if you can determine its limits.

```
TO POLYGON
;
;--- INITIALIZE SCREEN AND TURTLE ---
;
CS PD HT SETH 90
;
;PRINT PROMPT
;
PRINT [Enter number of]
PRINT [sides and press]
PRINT [RETURN]
;
;--- GET NUMBER ---
;
MAKE "A READQUOTE
;
```

```
;--- DRAW POLYGON ---
;
REPEAT :A [FD 200 / :A LT 360 / :A]
END
```

Shapes

In the previous section, you saw a procedure that drew symmetrical polygons. As you may have discovered, if you enter more than 20 for the number of sides, the result resembles a circle.

Although you can use these kinds of commands to draw almost any shape, ST LOGO has some built-in shape commands that make drawing certain shapes much easier.

BOX

The basic form of the BOX command is

BOX [x y w h]

where x is the horizontal location of the lower-left corner of the box, y is the vertical location of the lower-left corner of the box, w is the width, and h is the height.

The BOX command draws a rectangle at a specified location in the window, regardless of the location of the turtle. With this command you can specify the size, form and location of the shape without moving the turtle. This makes drawing much faster than drawing with the turtle. Try this procedure:

```
TO RECTS
CS ST
MAKE "GFILL "FALSE
MAKE "J 0
LABEL "NEWBOX
MAKE "J :J + 1
IF :J = 15 [GO "FIN]
MAKE "A (RANDOM 100) - 50
MAKE "B SENTENCE :A (RANDOM 100) - 50
MAKE "C SENTENCE :B RANDOM 50
MAKE "D SENTENCE :C RANDOM 50
BOX :D
GO "NEWBOX
LABEL "FIN
END
```

Here the turtle is always in the center of the window, but the rectangles are drawn at various unrelated locations in the window.

Notice that the X and Y coordinates specify the location of the lower-left corner of the rectangle.

CIRCLE

The basic form of the CIRCLE command is

CIRCLE [x y r]

where x is the horizontal location of the center of the circle, y is the vertical position of the center of the circle, and r is the radius of the circle.

The CIRCLE command draws circles. You specify the center of the circle with the X and Y coordinates and the radius. Try this procedure:

```
TO CIRCS
CS ST
MAKE "GFILL "FALSE
MAKE "J 0
LABEL "NEWCIRCLE
MAKE "J :J + 1
IF :J = 15 [GO "FIN]
MAKE "A (RANDOM 100) - 50
MAKE "B SENTENCE :A (RANDOM 100) - 50
MAKE "C SENTENCE :B RANDOM 50
CIRCLE :C
GO "NEWCIRCLE
LABEL "FIN
END
```

As in the BOX procedure, the turtle is always in the center of the window, but the circles are drawn at various unrelated locations in the window.

ARC

The basic form of the ARC command is

ARC [x y r b e]

where x is the horizontal location of the arc, y is the vertical position of the arc, and r is its radius.

The ARC command draws portions of a circle. You specify the circle that contains the arc with the X and Y coordinates and the radius. The b and e specifications determine the beginning and ending angles of the arc. Try this procedure:

```
?TO ARCS
CS ST
MAKE "GFILL "TRUE
SETFILL [0 1 1]
MAKE "J 0
LABEL "NEWARC
MAKE "J :J + 1
IF :J = 15 [GO "FIN]
MAKE "A (RANDOM 100) - 50
```

```
MAKE "B SENTENCE :A (RANDOM 100) - 50
MAKE "C SENTENCE :B RANDOM 100
MAKE "D SENTENCE :C RANDOM 360
MAKE "E SENTENCE :D RANDOM 360
ARC :E
GO "NEWARC
LABEL "FIN
END
```

ELLIPSE

Ellipses are stretched or flattened circles. The basic form of the ELLIPSE command is

ELLIPSE [x y xr yr]

where x is the horizontal location of the center of the ellipse, y is the vertical position of the center of the ellipse, xr is its radius in the horizontal direction, and yr is its radius in the vertical direction. Here is an example:

```
TO ELLPS
CS ST
MAKE "GFILL "FALSE
MAKE "J 0
LABEL "NEWELLIPSE
MAKE "J :J + 1
IF :J = 15 [GO "FIN]
MAKE "A (RANDOM 100) - 50
MAKE "B SENTENCE :A (RANDOM 100) - 50
MAKE "C SENTENCE :B RANDOM 50
MAKE "D SENTENCE :C RANDOM 50
ELLIPSE :D
GO "NEWELLIPSE
LABEL "FIN
END
```

POLY

POLY creates a shape that is made up of a list of coordinates. It allows you to easily draw irregular shapes in almost any size. The basic form of the POLY command is

POLY [coordinate-x coordinate-y coordinate-x coordinate-y. . .]

where each pair of x and y coordinates specifies the next point of the polygon. Here is an example:

```
TO POLYS
CS HT
MAKE "C "
MAKE "A (RANDOM 10) + 3
LABEL "NEXTPOINT
```

```
IF :A = 0 [GO "FIN]
MAKE "B (RANDOM 100) - 50
MAKE "C SENTENCE :B :C
MAKE "B (RANDOM 100) - 50
MAKE "C SENTENCE :B :C
MAKE "A :A - 1
GO "NEXTPOINT
LABEL "FIN
MAKE "C BUTLAST :C
POLY :C
END
```

FILL

All of the shapes you have drawn so far are hollow. The FILL command fills the inside of any shape, making it solid.

Solid Colors

There are two ways to use FILL. If FILL is active, it will automatically fill any of the built-in shapes (CIRCLE, ELLIPSE, BOX and ARC). To turn on the FILL function, you either can select Graphics from the Settings menu and click on the True box for FILL:

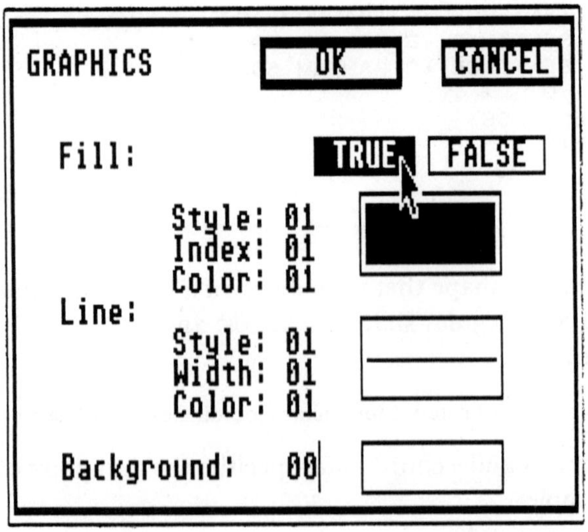

or you can enter the command

MAKE “GFILL “TRUE

directly from the keyboard. Make FILL true, and then try the following example:

```
TO FILL_EXAMPLES
CS HT
FILL_ARC
FILL_CIRCLE
FILL_BOX
END

TO FILL_CIRCLE
MAKE "GFILL "TRUE
CIRCLE [0 120 50]
END

TO FILL_BOX
MAKE "GFILL "TRUE
BOX [70 -30 50 20]
END

TO FILL_ARC
MAKE "GFILL "TRUE
ARC [-100 -50 50 20 270]
END
```

In addition to automatically filling the built-in shapes, FILL can fill any manually drawn shape. In the following example, FILL has been added to the POLYGON procedure from earlier in this chapter:

```
TO POLYGON
;
;--- INITIALIZE SCREEN AND TURTLE ---
;
CS PD HT SETH 90
;
;PRINT PROMPT
;
PRINT [Enter number of]
PRINT [sides and press]
PRINT [RETURN]
;
;--- GET NUMBER ---
;
MAKE "A READQUOTE
;
;--- DRAW POLYGON ---
;
REPEAT :A [FD 200 / :A LT 360 / :A]
;
;FILL POLYGON
;
```

```
MAKE "GFILL "TRUE
SETFILL [1 1 1]
LT 30 PU FD 5 FILL
END
```

You have to move the turtle inside the shape to be filled; unlike the built-in shape commands, FILL is linked to the turtle's location. If you execute FILL while the turtle is outside the desired shape, you will fill the background.

```
RIGHT 30 PENUP FORWARD 5 FILL
```

Patterns

There are two kinds of patterns that the ST can produce: fill patterns and line patterns. The ST has 7 built-in line patterns and 36 built-in fill patterns. The following procedure displays all of the built-in line patterns:

```
TO LINE_PATTERN
CS HT PU
SETPOS [-60 -40]
PD
TT [SETLINE []
PU SETPOS [28 -40]
PD TT [1 1]
PU SETPOS [58 -40]
PD TT "]
MAKE "A 1
MAKE "B 1
MAKE "C 1
LABEL "LOOP
MAKE "D SENTENCE :A :B
MAKE "D SENTENCE :D :C
SETLINE :D
PU SETPOS [-60 -20]
PE SETH 90
FD 120
PD BK 120
PU
SETPOS [13 -40]
PX
TT :A
REPEAT 20 [MAKE "Q 10]
MAKE "A :A + 1
IF :A = 8 [GO "FIN]
```

LINE PATTERNS

The SETLINE command has three parameters. The first changes the line pattern, the second changes the line width, and the third changes the line color. The patterns only apply to lines with a width of 1. When you run this routine, all seven of the patterns will be displayed in the Graphics Display window with their associated SETLINE parameters just below the displayed line.

To change line width, you must enter values into the second variable. The following routing displays lines that are from 1 to 39 dots wide:

```
TO LINE_WIDTH
CS HT PU
SETPOS [-60 -40]
PD
TT [SETLINE [1]
PU SETPOS [50 -40]
PD TT "1
PU SETPOS [58 -40]
PD TT "]
MAKE "A 1
MAKE "B 1
MAKE "C 1
LABEL "LOOP
MAKE "D SENTENCE :A :B
MAKE "D SENTENCE :D :C
SETLINE :D
PU SETPOS [-60 -10]
PE SETH 90
FD 120
PD BK 120
PU
SETPOS [27 -40]
PX
TT :B
REPEAT 20 [MAKE "Q 10]
MAKE "B :B + 2
IF :B = 41 [GO "FIN]
TT :B - 2
GO "LOOP
LABEL "FIN
END
```

FILL PATTERNS

There are two different kinds of fill patterns: pictorial and cross-hatch patterns. Of the built-in patterns, 24 are pictorial and 12 are cross-hatch. The following procedure displays the cross-hatch patterns and their associated parameters:

```
TO HATCH_PATTERN
CS HT PU
SETPOS [-60 -40]
PD
TT [SETFILL [1]
PU SETPOS [46 -40]
```

```
PD TT "1
PU SETPOS [54 -40]
PD TT "]
MAKE "A 1
MAKE "B 1
MAKE "C 1
LABEL "LOOP
MAKE "D SENTENCE :A :B
MAKE "D SENTENCE :D :C
SETFILL :D
PU SETPOS [-30 -30]
SETH 90
PE
FD 60
PD
BK 60
PU
SETPOS [25 -40]
PX
TT :B
REPEAT 20 [MAKE "Q 10]
MAKE "A :A + 1
IF :A = 8 [GO "FIN]
TT :A - 1
GO "LOOP
LABEL "FIN
END
```

Notice that the first parameter in the cross-hatch command is 3. To display the pictorial patterns, the first parameter must be 2:

```
TO PICT_PATTERN
CS HT PU
MAKE "GFILL "TRUE
SETLINE [1 1 1]
SETPOS [-60 -40]
PD
TT [SETFILL [1]
PU SETPOS [46 -40]
PD TT "1
PU SETPOS [54 -40]
PD TT "]
MAKE "A 2
MAKE "B 1
MAKE "C 1
LABEL "LOOP
MAKE "D SENTENCE :A :B
MAKE "D SENTENCE :D :C
SETFILL :D
BOX [-30 -20 60 60]
PU
SETPOS [25 -40]
PX
TT :B
REPEAT 20 [MAKE "Q 10]
```

```
MAKE "B :B + 1
IF :B = 25 [GO "FIN]
TT :B - 1
GO "LOOP
LABEL "FIN
END
```

You may also select any combination of pattern parameters for both line and fill patterns from Graphics choice in the Settings menu.

There are six controls in this window:

- Fill TRUE/FALSE
- Fill Color
- Line Style
- Line Width
- Line Color
- Background Color.

To change the values, use the mouse pointer or the arrow keys to position the cursor to the right of the item you wish to change. Then press the DELETE key and retype the values. When you are done, click the OK box to make the selected changes or click the Cancel box to abandon the changes.

Custom Patterns

The ST has a preprogrammed, customized fill pattern in addition to the built-in patterns. The following procedure displays this pattern:

```
TO CUSTOM_PATTERN
CS HT PU
SETPOS [-60 -40]
PD
TT [SETFILL [4]
PU SETPOS [46 -40]
PD TT "1
PU SETPOS [54 -40]
PD TT "]
MAKE "A 4
MAKE "B 1
MAKE "C 1
LABEL "LOOP
MAKE "D SENTENCE :A :B
MAKE "D SENTENCE :D :C
SETFILL :D
BOX [-30 -30 60 60]
PU
SETPOS [25 -40]
PX
```

```
TT :B
REPEAT 20 [MAKE "Q 10]
MAKE "B :B + 1
IF :B = 2 [GO "FIN]
TT :B - 1
GO "LOOP
LABEL "FIN
END
```

FILL PATTERNS

The form of a custom fill pattern is

PPROP "GRAPHICS ".FPT [n1 n2 n3 n4 n5 n6 n7 n8 n9
n10 n11 n12 n13 n14 n15 n16]

where n1 through n16 are numbers between 0 and 65535. The actual pattern that will appear consists of 16 lines of dots (either white or black, or the current programmed color). The dot patterns on each line are binary representations of the numbers you enter. For example, the pattern is made up of the following numbers:

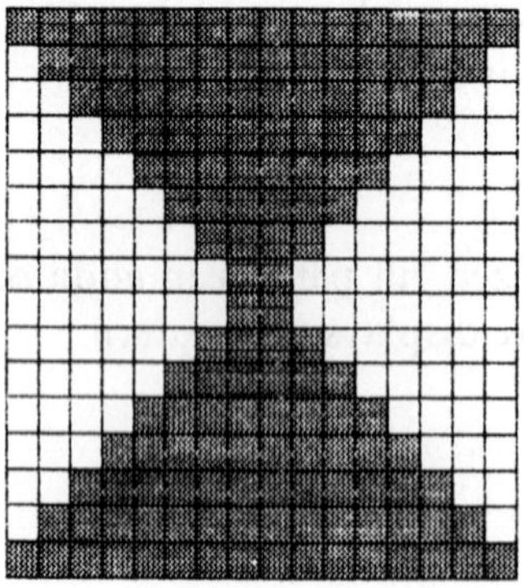

```
1 1 1 1 1 1 1 1 1 1 1 1 1 1 1 1
0 1 1 1 1 1 1 1 1 1 1 1 1 1 1 0
0 0 1 1 1 1 1 1 1 1 1 1 1 1 0 0
0 0 0 1 1 1 1 1 1 1 1 1 1 0 0 0
0 0 0 0 1 1 1 1 1 1 1 1 0 0 0 0
0 0 0 0 0 1 1 1 1 1 1 0 0 0 0 0
0 0 0 0 0 0 1 1 1 1 0 0 0 0 0 0
0 0 0 0 0 0 0 1 1 0 0 0 0 0 0 0
0 0 0 0 0 0 0 1 1 0 0 0 0 0 0 0
0 0 0 0 0 0 1 1 1 1 0 0 0 0 0 0
0 0 0 0 0 1 1 1 1 1 1 0 0 0 0 0
0 0 0 0 1 1 1 1 1 1 1 1 0 0 0 0
0 0 0 1 1 1 1 1 1 1 1 1 1 0 0 0
0 0 1 1 1 1 1 1 1 1 1 1 1 1 0 0
0 1 1 1 1 1 1 1 1 1 1 1 1 1 1 0
1 1 1 1 1 1 1 1 1 1 1 1 1 1 1 1
```

The decimal equivalents of these binary numbers are

```
65535
32766
16380
8184
4080
2016
960
384
384
960
2016
```

```
4080
8184
16380
32766
65535
```

The easiest way to produce patterns is to draw the patterns on a 16×16 grid, coloring in the squares that correspond to the pattern you want. The previous illustration is an example of a grid and pattern. Once you have designed your pattern, you'll need to convert the dots to 1's (the dark squares) and 0's (the white squares).

After you have converted your pattern into binary numbers, you can use the following procedure to convert the binary numbers into their decimal equivalents:

```
TO BIN_DEC
CS HT PU
SETPOS [-140 100]
PD
TT [ENTER A SIXTEEN DIGIT BINARY NUMBER]
PU
MAKE "NP -60
SETPOS [-60 30]
PD
TT [________________]
MAKE "TOTAL 0
PU
SETPOS [-40 -100]
PD
TT :TOTAL
PU
SETPOS [-100 -40]
PD
TT [DECIMAL VALUE:]
PU
MAKE "MULTIPLIER 32768
;
LABEL "NEXTDIGIT
;
; --- CURSOR ---
MAKE "NEWPOSITION SENTENCE :NP 30
SETPOS :NEWPOSITION
PX
TT "_
TT "=
;
LABEL "READ_DIGIT
;
MAKE "DIGIT READCHAR
IF OR (:DIGIT > 1) (:DIGIT < 0) [GO "READ_DIGIT]
TT "=
TT :DIGIT
;
```

```
; --- ADD TO TOTAL ---
;
MAKE "DELTOTAL :TOTAL
MAKE "TOTAL :TOTAL + (:DIGIT * :MULTIPLIER)
MAKE "MULTIPLIER :MULTIPLIER / 2
IF :MULTIPLIER < 1 [GO "FIN]
MAKE "NP (:NP + 8)
PU
SETPOS [-40 -100]
PX
TT :DELTOTAL
TT :TOTAL
PU
GO "NEXTDIGIT
LABEL "FIN
PU
SETPOS [-40 -100]
PX
TT :DELTOTAL
TT :TOTAL
END
```

Once you have derived the decimal values for your pattern, enter the decimal numbers into a PPROP command. If you want to see how your new pattern looks, clear the screen with the CS command and give the fill command.

LINE PATTERNS

Like fill patterns, you can create custom line patterns. The form of a custom line pattern is

PPROP "GRAPHICS ".LPT n

where n is any decimal number between 0 and 65535. The process of writing the pattern for a line is the same as for writing a single line of a fill pattern. Use the previous procedure to determine the decimal value that corresponds to the binary pattern, and enter it into the PPROP line above.

COLOR

If you are using an ST with a monochrome monitor, you may wish to skip this section and go on to the next chapter. If you have a color monitor, the first thing you should do before continuing is to set the display to low resolution. You will then have 16 colors with which to draw and paint.

The ST can produce 512 different colors—as many as 16 at one time. These colors can be chosen for the background, characters, shapes, text, and fill patterns that the ST puts on the screen, and each of these can be set independently. When the ST is first turned on, the lines and text are black and the background is white. You can change these colors with keyboard commands or through the Settings menu.

Open the Graphics control window again from the Settings menu. You will be looking at the numeric controls for the fill, line, and background functions.

To modify the colors from the keyboard or from within a procedure, give the SETLINE or SETFILL command, selecting the color you want and inserting its value into the third parameter. The colors available in the initial color palette are as follows:

0	White	8	Light Gray
1	Black	9	Dark Gray
2	Red	10	Light Turquoise
3	Light Green	11	Turquoise
4	Light Blue	12	Light Purple
5	Blue	13	Purple
6	Brown	14	Yellow
7	Green	15	Olive Green

The fill color affects shapes that you paint with the FILL command as well as areas that you fill with patterns.

```
TO COLORS
CS ST
MAKE "GFILL "TRUE
MAKE "X RANDOM 4
MAKE "Y SENTENCE [1 1] :X
SETFILL :Y
MAKE "J 0
LABEL "NEWARC
MAKE "J :J + 1
IF :J = 15 [GO "FIN]
MAKE "A (RANDOM 100) - 50
MAKE "B SENTENCE :A (RANDOM 100) - 50
MAKE "C SENTENCE :B RANDOM 100
MAKE "D SENTENCE :C RANDOM 360
MAKE "E SENTENCE :D RANDOM 360
MAKE "GFILL "TRUE
MAKE "X RANDOM 4
MAKE "Y SENTENCE [1 1] :X
SETFILL :Y
```

```
ARC :E
GO "NEWARC
LABEL "FIN
END
```

The line color affects any text that you display in the Graphics Display window by using TURTLETEXT, as well as any lines or shapes that you draw with the turtle.

```
?TO COLORLINES
MAKE "X 0
PD HT CS
LABEL "LOOP
MAKE "X :X + 1
MAKE "C (RANDOM 200) - 100
MAKE "D (RANDOM 200) - 100
MAKE "E SENTENCE :C :D
MAKE "A RANDOM 4
MAKE "B SENTENCE [2 1] :A
SETLINE :B
SETPOS :E
IF :X > 20 [GO "FIN]
GO "LOOP
LABEL "FIN
PRINT "DONE
END
```

Here, for example, is a procedure that draws a red circle inside a green square in the center of a black window:

```
TO PICT
SETBG 1
CS PU HT
MAKE "GFILL "TRUE
SETFILL [1 1 3]
BOX [-80 -80 160 160]
SETFILL [1 1 2]
CIRCLE [0 0 60]
END
```

Mixing Colors

There are two ways to mix new colors for your palette. The easiest way is to use the control panel, because you can see the colors change as you mix them. To access the control panel, pull down the Desk menu until the words "Control Panel" are highlighted, and click the mouse button once.

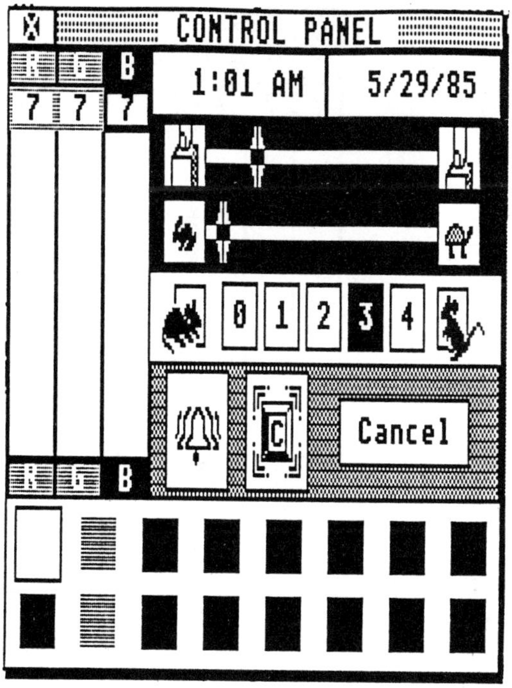

If you look along the bottom of the Control Panel, you will see the 16 palette colors. They are numbered as follows:

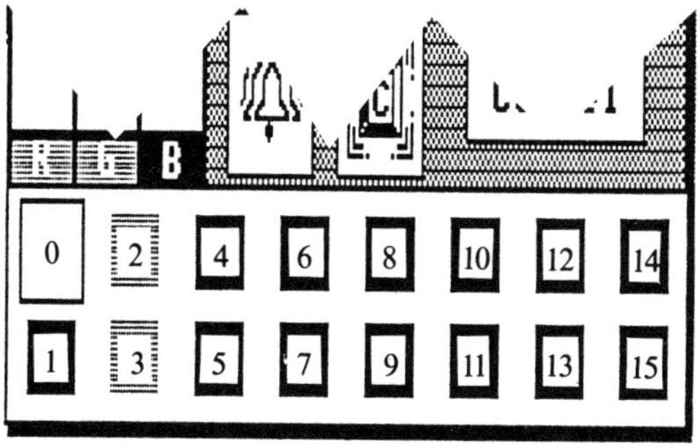

When you first open the Control Panel, color 0 (white) is selected—it has a large box around it. To select a different color just click on its box. To modify a selected color, move the color control levers along the left side of the Control Panel.

There are two ways you can move these levers: you can drag them with the mouse pointer or click in the Color boxes at the top and bottom of the control levers.

To select another color, click on its Color box in the palette. When you are done you can either close the Control Panel to save your changes or click in the Cancel box to restore the former color palette.

Changing Colors From the Keyboard

To change the palette colors from the keyboard, use the SETPAL command. The basic form of a SETPAL command is

SETPAL c [n1 n2 n3]

where c is the number of the color you want to change and n1, n2 and n3 are the RGB values you want to put into the new color. For example, the line

```
?SETPAL 2 [1000 700 0]
```

will make palette color 2 gold. To check the values of a color, you can use the PAL command. For example, to check the values we just put into palette color 2, enter the line **PAL 2**. Notice that the numbers you get from the ST do not match the numbers we put into the palette. There are only eight color steps in each of the primary colors; these are 1000, 857, 714, 571, 428, 285, 142, and 0.

To compensate for this (and so you won't have to memorize these strange values), the ST automatically selects valid color numbers that are the closest to the numbers you enter.

CHAPTER

LOGO Primitives 7

The 520-ST can use a great number of functional operations directly from LOGO—in fact, there are more than 150 LOGO primitives. These include mathematical derivations, screen formatting instructions, string and list manipulators, file controls, and graphics commands. They are presented here in alphabetical order. Abbreviations are listed in parentheses after the name.

ABS

Definition

Computes the absolute (positive) value of a number.

Example

```
MAKE "A ABS 100
100
MAKE "A ABS -100
100
```

AND

Definition

Examines the results of two comparisons and responds with TRUE if they are both true.

Example

```
MAKE "A 123
MAKE "B 100 + 23
MAKE "C 40
AND (:A = :B) (:C = 40)
TRUE
```

ARC

Definition

Draws a section of a circle between two angles specified in degrees.

Form

ARC x,y,r,b,e

where x and y specify the center of the circle that defines the arc, r is the radius, b is the beginning angle, and e is the ending angle.

Example

```
ARC [100 100 30 0 150]
```

ARCTAN

Definition

Calculates the arctangent of a number.

Example

```
ARCTAN 45
88.726978
```

ASCII

Definition

Computes the ASCII value of a character. If more than one character is input (for example, a word), this primitive computes the value of the first character in the word.

Example

```
MAKE "A "HELLO
MAKE "B "A
ASCII :A
72
ASCII :B
65
ASCII "P
80
```

BACK

Definition

Moves the turtle the specified number of dots away from the direction it is pointed.

Example

```
BACK 100
```

BOX

Definition

Draws a rectangle.

Form

BOX x,y,w,h

where x and y are the coordinates of the lower-left corner of the box, w is the width, and h is the height of the box.

Example

```
BOX [100 100 50 70]
```

BURY

Definition

Protects a "package" of procedures from being edited (*see also* PACKAGE).

Example

```
BURY "PACKAGE.NAM
```

BUTFIRST (BF)

Definition

Deletes the first item from a string. If the string is a word, BUTFIRST removes the first character. If the string is a sentence made up of several words, BUTFIRST removes the first word.

Example

```
MAKE "A "THE QUICK BROWN FOX
MAKE "B "ABCDEFG
PRINT BUTFIRST :A
QUICK BROWN FOX
PRINT BUTFIRST :B
BCDEFG
```

BUTLAST (BL)

Definition

Deletes the last item from a string. If the string is a word, BUTLAST removes the last character. If the string is a sentence made up of several words, BUTLAST removes the last word.

Example

```
MAKE "A "THE QUICK BROWN FOX
MAKE "B "ABCDEFG
PRINT BUTLAST :A
THEF QUICK BROWN
PRINT BUTLAST :B
ABCDEF
```

BYE

Definition

Ends LOGO and returns to the ST's opening windows.

CATCH

Definition

Intercepts errors that would interrupt a program and display an Error box. Allows you to perform your own error-handling.

Example

```
TO CATCH_ERROR
CATCH "ERROR [TEST_PROC]
PRINT [TRY AGAIN]
RUN [TEST_PROC]
END

TO TEST_PROC
LABEL "GET_NEXT_VALUES
PRINT [ENTER TWO NUMBERS]
MAKE "A READLIST
MAKE "B SENTENCE :A [100 100]
BOX :B
GO "GET_NEXT_VALUES
END
```

CHANGEF

Definition

Renames a file on the disk.

Example

```
CHANGEF "NEWNAME OLDNAME
```

CHAR

Definition

Returns the ASCII character equivalent of a number.

Example

```
TO CONVERT
MAKE "A 65
LABEL "NEXT_CHARACTER
TYPE :A TYPE CHAR 32 PRINT CHAR :A
MAKE "A :A + 1
IF :A > 255 [OUTPUT "DONE]
GO "NEXT_CHARACTER
END
```

CIRCLE

Definition

Draws a circle.

Form

CIRCLE x,y,r

where x and y specify the center of the circle and r is the radius.

Example

```
CIRCLE [0 0 100]
```

CLEAN

Definition

Erases everything except the turtle from the Graphics Display window. Leaves the turtle in its current location and heading.

Example

```
CLEAN
```

CLEARSCREEN (CS)

Definition

Erases everything except the turtle from the Graphics Display window. Returns the turtle to its home position and heading (typically, the center of the Graphics Display window, pointing straight up).

Example

```
CLEARSCREEN
```

CLEARTEXT (CT)

Definition

Erases everything from the LOGO Dialog window and returns the text cursor to the upper-left corner of the window.

Example

```
CLEARTEXT
```

CO

Definition

Returns control to a procedure halted by PAUSE.

Example

```
CO
```

COPYDEF

Definition

Creates a new procedure with a name that is different from the original procedure.

Example

```
COPYDEF "NEWNAME "OLDNAME
```

COPYOFF

Definition

Terminates a COPYON command.

Example

```
COPYOFF
```

COPYON

Definition

Sends a copy of all text to both the printer and the screen.

Example

```
COPYON
```

COS

Definition

Calculates the cosine of a number.

Example

```
COS 45
0.707107
```

COUNT

Definition

Calculates the length of a string.

Example

```
MAKE "A [HELLO THERE]
MAKE "B "HELLO_THERE
COUNT :A
2
COUNT :B
11
```

DEFINE

Definition

Creates a one-line procedure. Similar to the TO primitive, which produces multi-line procedures.

Example

```
DEFINE "PENTAGON [[][CS SETH 90 REPEAT 5 [FD 50 LT 72]]
```

DEFINEDP

Definition

Determines if a specified string is the name of a procedure in the workspace.

Example

```
DEFINEDP "PENTAGON
TRUE
```

DEGREES

Definition

Converts radians to degrees.

Example

```
DEGREES 45
2578.310251
```

DIR

Definition

Displays a list of all the LOGO file names on the currently logged disk.

Example

```
DIR
[PROC_1.LOG PROC_2.LOG]
```

EDALL

Definition

Puts a copy of everything in the workspace into the Edit window so that it can be modified.

Example

```
EDALL
```

EDF

Definition

Reads a file from the disk and puts it into the Edit window so that it can be modified.

Example

```
EDF "PROC_1
```

EDIT (ED)

Definition

Puts a copy of a procedure that is in memory into the Edit window so that it can be modified.

Example

```
EDIT "PROC_1
```

EDNS

Definition

Puts a copy of all the variables in memory into the Edit window so they can be modified.

Example

```
EDNS
EDNS VAR_1
```

EDPS

Definition

Puts a copy of all the procedures in memory into the Edit window so they can be modified.

Example

```
EDPS
EDPS "PROC_1
```

ELLIPSE

Definition

Draws an ellipse.

Form

ELLIPSE x, y, rx, ry

where x and y specify the center of the ellipse, rx is the horizontal radius, and ry is the vertical radius.

Example

```
ELLIPSE [0 0 100 150]
```

EMPTYP

Definition

Checks for the definition of a specified word and returns TRUE if it is undefined.

Example

```
MAKE "A "HELLO
EMPTYP [A]
FALSE
EMPTYP []
TRUE
```

END

Definition

Specifies the last line in a procedure. LOGO requires that every procedure end with the word END. If you edit a procedure and forget to add END, LOGO will add it for you.

EQUALP

Definition

Compares two strings. If they are the same, EQUALP returns TRUE.

Example

```
MAKE "A "HELLO
MAKE "B "THERE
MAKE "C SENTENCE :A :B
EQUALP (SENTENCE :A :B) :C
TRUE
```

ERALL

Definition

Erases everything from memory except those procedures that are part of buried packages.

ERASE (ER)

Definition

Similar to ERALL, except ERASE only erases the specified procedures from memory.

Example

```
ERASE "PROC_1
```

ERASEFILE

Definition

Erases a file from currently logged disk.

Example

```
ERASEFILE "DISKFILE_1
```

ERN

Definition

Erases defined variables from memory.

Example

```
MAKE "A "ONE
MAKE "B "TWO
MAKE "C "THREE
POALL
C is THREE
B is TWO
```

```
A Is ONE
ERN [A B C]
POALL
```

ERNS

Definition

Erases all variables that have been stored in memory.

ERPS

Definition

Similar to ERASE, but also erases procedures within packages.

Example

```
ERPS
```

ERROR

Definition

Reprints the most recent LOGO error message.

EXP

Definition

Calculates the natural exponent of a number.

Example

```
EXP 100
9.223371E18
```

FENCE

Definition

Creates a boundary that traces the inside of the Graphics Display window. Trying to draw outside of the fenced area will generate an error.

FILL

Definition

Fills an area with the current pattern and color. The area to be filled begins at the current location of the turtle.

Example

```
TO FILL_CIRCLE
MAKE "GFILL "FALSE
CS HT
CIRCLE [0 0 100]
PU
SETPOS [0 0]
PD
MAKE "GFILL "TRUE
SETFILL [1 1 1]
FILL
END
```

FILLATTR

Definition

Displays the current color and pattern values of FILL.

FIRST

Definition

Returns the first item in a string. If the string is a single word, FIRST returns the first character of the word. If the string is a sentence made of several words, FIRST returns the first word in the sentence.

Example

```
MAKE "A [THE QUICK BROWN FOX]
MAKE "B "123456789
PRINT FIRST :A
THE
PRINT FIRST :B
1
```

FORWARD (FD)

Definition

Moves the turtle a specified number of dots in the direction in which it is pointed.

Example

```
FORWARD 100
```

FPUT

Definition

Makes a single string out of two strings, placing the first string in front of the second.

Example

```
MAKE "A "HELLO
MAKE "B "THERE
MAKE "C FPUT :A :B
```

GETTEXT

Definition

Returns the value of the current text style.

Example

```
GETTEXT
0
```

GO

Definition

Makes the procedure jump to the line with the specified label.

Example

```
MAKE "A 0
LABEL "LOOP
PRINT :A
MAKE "A :A + 1
IF :A > 10 [OUTPUT "DONE]
GO "LOOP
END
```

GPROP

Definition

Returns a list of the values of the specified item's properties.

Example

```
PPROP "HOUSE "WINDOW "OPEN
GPROP "HOUSE "WINDOW
OPEN
```

HEADING

Definition

Responds with the turtle's current direction in degrees.

HIDETURTLE (HT)

Definition

Causes the turtle to disappear from the Graphics Display window.

HOME

Definition

Places the turtle at the x,y location (0,0), which is usually the center of the Graphics Display window, and sets its heading to 0 (straight up).

IF

Definition

Examines a logical statement. If it is true, IF causes the procedure to execute the statement that immediately follows and to skip the next statement. If the statement is false, IF causes the procedure to skip the statement that immediately follows it and continue execution with the next statement.

Example

```
MAKE "A 0
LABEL "LOOP
PRINT :A
MAKE "A :A + 1
IF :A > 10 [OUTPUT "DONE]
GO "LOOP
END
```

INT

Definition

Returns the integer of a number (the nondecimal portion).

Example

```
MAKE "A 7
MAKE "B 3
PRINT :A/:B
2.333333
PRINT INT :A/:B
2
```

ITEM

Definition

Returns the selected item from a string. If the string is a single word, the item returned will be a single character. If the string is a sentence made up of several words, ITEM will return a selected word.

Example

```
MAKE "A [THE QUICK BROWN FOX]
MAKE "B "123456789
PRINT ITEM 1 :A
THE
PRINT ITEM 1 :B
1
```

KEYP

Definition

Checks the keyboard buffer. If there is a character in the buffer (that is, a character has been typed), KEYP returns TRUE.

LABEL

Definition

Specifies a location within a procedure.

Example

```
MAKE "A 0
LABEL "LOOP
PRINT :A
MAKE "A :A + 1
IF :A > 10 [OUTPUT "DONE]
GO "LOOP
END
```

LAST

Definition

Returns the last item in a string. If the string is a single word, LAST returns the last character of the word. If the string is a sentence, LAST returns the last word in the sentence.

Example

```
MAKE "A [THE QUICK BROWN FOX]
MAKE "B "123456789
PRINT LAST :A
FOX
PRINT LAST :B
9
```

LEFT (LT)

Definition

Turns the turtle a specified number of degrees counterclockwise.

Example

```
LEFT 100
```

LINEATTR

Definition

Displays the current color and pattern values of LINE.

LIST

Definition

Prints the values of variables.

Example

```
MAKE "A "HELLO
MAKE "B "THERE
LIST :A :B
[HELLO THERE]
```

LISTP

Definition

Returns TRUE if the item is the name of a list.

Example

```
LISTP "PROC_1
FALSE
```

LOAD

Definition

Loads a LOGO file into the workspace from the disk.

Example

```
LOAD "PROC_1
```

LOADPIC

Definition

Loads the contents of a picture file into the Graphics Display window.

Example

```
LOADPIC "LPICTURE.PIC
```

LOG

Definition

Calculates the natural logarithm of a number.

Example

```
LOG 100
4.60517
```

LOG10

Definition

Calculates the base 10 logarithm of a number.

Example

```
LOG10 100
2
```

LOWERCASE (LC)

Definition

Converts all the alphabetic characters of a string into lowercase letters.

Example

```
LOWERCASE "THE
the
```

LPUT

Definition

Makes a single string out of two strings, placing the first string after the second.

Example

```
MAKE "A "HELLO
MAKE "B "THERE
MAKE "C LPUT :A :B
PRINT :A :B :C
HELLO
THERE
HELLOTHERE
```

MAKE

Definition

Creates a new list. The first word following MAKE is the name of the list, and the items that follow are the contents of the list.

Example

```
MAKE "A "HELLO
MAKE "B "THERE
PRINT :A :B
HELLO
THERE
```

MEMBERP

Definition

Returns TRUE if the first word or character is a subset of the second.

Example

```
MAKE "A "HELLO
MAKE "B "THERE
MAKE "C FPUT :A :B
MEMBERP :A :C
TRUE
MEMBERP :C :A
FALSE
```

MOUSE

Definition

Returns the current position and condition of the mouse. The items are

X, Y, LB, RB, IGDW

where x and y are the horizontal and vertical coordinates of the mouse position, LB is the status of the left button, RB is the status of the right button, and IGDW indicates if the mouse is inside the Graphics Display window.

Example

```
MOUSE
[-77 -11.005916 FALSE FALSE TRUE]
```

NAME

Definition

Creates a new list. The last word in the list is the name of the list, and the items that precede it are the contents of the list.

Example

```
NAME "HELLO "A
:A
HELLO
```

NAMEP

Definition

Returns TRUE if the item is the name of a variable.

Example

```
MAKE "A "HELLO
NAME "THERE "B
NAMEP "A
TRUE
NAMEP "B
TRUE
NAMEP "C
FALSE
```

NODES

Definition

Calculates the amount of unused memory in the ST. One NODE is equal to four bytes.

Example

```
TO FREE_MEM
TYPE [YOU HAVE] TYPE CHAR 32
TYPE NODES * 4 TYPE CHAR 32
PRINT [BYTES FREE]
END
FREE_MEM
YOU HAVE 26364 BYTES FREE
```

NOFORMAT

Definition

Deletes all of the comments in memory.

NOT

Definition

Returns the opposite logical value of the statement.

Example

```
MAKE "A "HELLO
NAME "THERE "B
NAMEP "A
TRUE
NOT NAMEP "A
FALSE
```

NOTRACE

Definition

Disables the TRACE debugging feature.

NOWATCH

Definition

Disables the WATCH debugging feature.

NUMBERP

Definition

Returns TRUE if the item is a number.

Example

```
MAKE "B 45
MAKE "A "HELLO
NUMBERP :A
FALSE
NUMBERP :B
TRUE
```

OR

Definition

Returns TRUE if either of two statements is true.

Example

```
MAKE "A 1
MAKE "B 2
OR (:A = 1) (:B = 2)
TRUE
OR (:A = 0) (:B = 2)
TRUE
OR (:A = 0) (:B = 0)
FALSE
OR (:A = 1) (:B = 0)
TRUE
```

OUTPUT (OP)

Definition

Ends a procedure and prints the string that follows OUTPUT.

Example

```
TO COUNT_UP
MAKE "A 0
LABEL "LOOP
PRINT :A
MAKE "A :A + 1
IF :A > 20 [OUTPUT "DONE]
GO LOOP
END
```

PACKAGE

Definition

Makes the named procedures part of the named package.

Example

```
PACKAGE "PACKAGENAME "PROC_1
```

PALETTE (PAL)

Definition

Responds with the red, green, and blue values for the specified palette color numbers.

PAUSE

Definition

Temporarily halts a procedure. The procedure is restarted with CO.

PENDOWN (PD)

Definition

Causes all subsequent turtle-movement commands to draw lines in the Graphics Display window.

PENERASE (PE)

Definition

Causes all subsequent turtle-movement commands to erase lines in the Graphics Display window.

PENREVERSE (PX)

Definition

Causes all subsequent turtle-movement commands to draw lines in the Graphics Display window that are the opposite color of the existing graphics.

PENUP (PU)

Definition

Prevents all subsequent turtle-movement commands from drawing lines in the Graphics Display window.

PI

Definition

Finds and displays the value of pi (3.1416).

PIECE

Definition

Selects items from a list.

Example

```
MAKE "A [THE QUICK BROWN FOX]
MAKE "B "123456789
PRINT PIECE 2 3 :A
QUICK BROWN
PRINT PIECE 2 5 :B
2345
```

PO

Definition

Prints out the contents of the selected procedure or the contents of the selected variable name.

Example

```
PO "COUNT_UP
TO COUNT_UP
MAKE "A 0
LABEL "LOOP
PRINT :A
MAKE "A :A + 1
IF :A > 20 [OUTPUT "DONE]
GO LOOP
END
```

POALL

Definition

Prints out the contents of all the procedures and the contents of all the variable names in memory.

Example

```
POALL
TO COUNT_UP
MAKE "A 0
LABEL "LOOP
PRINT :A
MAKE "A :A + 1
IF :A > 20 [OUTPUT "DONE]
GO LOOP
END

A Is 21
```

POLY

Definition

Performs a "connect-the-dots" function, joining all of the specified points with lines.

Example

```
TO POLYGON
CS HT
POLY [0 0 40 -50 1 67 -123 156 -98 -123 0 0]
```

PONS

Definition

Prints out the contents of all the variable names in memory.

POPKG

Definition

Prints out the names and contents of all the packages in memory.

POS

Definition

Returns the horizontal and vertical coordinates of the turtle's present location in the Graphics Display window.

PPROP

Definition

Assigns words to a property list.

Example

```
PPROP "HOUSE "DOOR "RED
PPS
HOUSE's DOOR is RED
```

PRINT (PR)

Definition

Puts the specified text in the LOGO Dialog window. PRINT always moves the text cursor to the beginning of the next line after printing.

Example

```
MAKE "A "HELLO
MAKE "B "THERE
MAKE "C [HELLO THERE]
PRINT :A
HELLO
PRINT :B
THERE
PRINT :C
[HELLO THERE]
```

QUOTIENT

Definition

Divides the first number by the second, and deletes any fractional part of the result.

Example

```
QUOTIENT 15 7
2
QUOTIENT 76 3
25
```

RADIANS

Definition

Converts degrees to radians.

Example

```
TO DEG_RAD
PRINT [ENTER RADIANS]
MAKE "A READQUOTE
MAKE "B RADIANS :A
TYPE :A TYPE CHAR 32 TYPE [RADIANS IS]
TYPE CHAR 32 TYPE :B TYPE CHAR 32
PRINT [DEGREES]
END
```

RANDOM

Definition

Generates a pseudorandom number between 0 and the specified number.

Example

```
PRINT RANDOM 2000
1765
```

READCHAR (RC)

Definition

Reads a character typed at the keyboard and assigns it to the specified variable.

Example

```
TO GUESS_NUMBER
PRINT [PICK A NUMBER BETWEEN 1 AND 9]
MAKE "A READCHAR
MAKE :B RANDOM 9
IF :A = :B [OUTPUT "RIGHT!]
PRINT [WRONG.]
END
```

READLIST (RL)

Definition

Reads a list typed at the keyboard and assigns it (including brackets) to the specified variable.

Example

```
TO SAY_HELLO
PRINT [ENTER YOUR NAME]
MAKE "A READLIST
SHOW [HELLO THERE]
SHOW :A
END

ENTER YOUR NAME
JOHN
[HELLO THERE]
[JOHN]
```

READQUOTE (RQ)

Definition

Reads a list typed at the keyboard and assigns it (without brackets) to the specified variable.

Example

```
TO SAY_HELLO
PRINT [ENTER YOUR NAME]
MAKE "A READQUOTE
SHOW [HELLO THERE]
SHOW :A
END
```

```
ENTER YOUR NAME
JOHN
[HELLO THERE]
JOHN
```

RECYCLE

Definition

Rearranges memory to remove any isolated memory space. This generally increases the amount of memory at your disposal.

REMAINDER

Definition

Divides the first number by the second, returning the integer remainder.

Example

```
QUOTIENT 15 7
2
QUOTIENT 76 3
25
REMAINDER 15 7
1
REMAINDER 76 3
1
```

REMPROP

Definition

Un-assigns a word or words from a specified property list.

Example

```
PPROP "HOUSE "DOOR "RED
PPS
HOUSE's DOOR is RED
REMPROP "HOUSE "DOOR "RED
PPS
[]
```

REPEAT

Definition

Performs a routine a specified number of times.

Example

```
TO "PENTAGON
CS SETH 90
REPEAT 5 [FD 50 LT 72]
```

RERANDOM

Definition

Causes the RANDOM and SHUFFLE primitives to generate the same pseudorandom number sequence repeatedly.

Example

```
TO SAME_DEAL
REPEAT 10 [TYPE RANDOM 10 TYPE CHAR 32]
PRINT CHAR 32
REPEAT 10 [RERANDOM TYPE RANDOM 10 TYPE CHAR 32]
PRINT CHAR 32
END

SAME_DEAL
6 2 9 0 3 1 6 2 3 7
6 6 6 6 6 6 6 6 6 6
```

RIGHT (RT)

Definition

Turns the turtle a specified number of degrees clockwise.

Example

```
RIGHT 100
```

ROUND

Definition

Calculates the integer of a number using rounding instead of truncation.

Example

```
TO ROUND/INT
LABEL "LOOP
MAKE "A READQUOTE
MAKE "B :A/7
```

```
PRINT :A
PRINT ROUND :B
PRINT INT :B
END

ROUND/INT
34
4.857143
5
4
```

SAVE

Definition

Saves the procedures and variables currently in memory on disk.

SAVEPIC

Definition

Saves the picture currently in the Graphics Display window on disk.

SCREENFACTS (SF)

Definition

Displays the current settings of the Graphics Display window. The data is

B, M, S, Z, X, Y

where B is the background color, M is the window mode (window, wrap, or fence), S is scrunch, Z is zoom, and X and Y are the pan values.

SENTENCE (SE)

Definition

Creates a string that contains the specified strings.

Example

```
MAKE "A "HELLO
MAKE "B "THERE
MAKE "C SENTENCE :A :B
PRINT :A
PRINT :B
PRINT :C
```

SETBG

Definition

Changes the background color of the Graphics Display window. To see the new color you need to execute a CLEARSCREEN command.

Example

```
TO SCRN_COL
MAKE :A 0
LABEL "LOOP
SETBG :A
CS
REPEAT 100 [MAKE "B 1]
MAKE "A :A +1
IF :A > 3 [OUTPUT "DONE!]
GO "LOOP
END
```

SETFILL

Definition

Changes the color and style of FILL. Does not affect colors and patterns already in the Graphics Display window.

Example

```
TO PATTERNS
CS HT
MAKE "A 1
LABEL "LOOP
MAKE "B SENTENCE :A [1]
MAKE "B SENTENCE [2] :B
SETFILL :B
MAKE "GFILL "TRUE
CS
CIRCLE [0 0 100]
MAKE "A :A + 1
IF :A > 12 [OUTPUT "DONE!]
REPEAT 10 [MAKE "B 1]
GO LOOP
END
```

SETHEADING (SETH)

Definition

Rotates the turtle so that it faces the direction (in degrees) specified.

Example

```
TO STAR
CS HT
MAKE "A 0
LABEL "LOOP
SETH RANDOM 360
FD RANDOM 100 HOME
MAKE "A :A + 1
IF :A > 30 [OUTPUT "DONE!]
GO "LOOP
END
```

SETLINE

Definition

Changes the color and style of a line. Does not affect colors and patterns of lines already in the Graphics Display window.

Example

```
TO LINE_STAR
CS HT
MAKE "A 0
LABEL "LOOP
MAKE "B SENTENCE :A [1]
MAKE "B SENTENCE [1] :B
SETLINE :B
SETH RANDOM 360
FD RANDOM 100 HOME
MAKE "A :A + 1
IF :A > 12 [GO PATS]
GO "LOOP
LABEL "PATS
CS HT
MAKE "A 0
LABEL "NEXTLOOP
MAKE "D RANDOM 7
MAKE "B SENTENCE :D [1 1]
SETLINE :B
SETH RANDOM 360
FD RANDOM 100 HOME
MAKE "A :A + 1
IF :A > 12 [OUTPUT "DONE!]
GO "NEXTLOOP
```

SETPAL

Definition

Changes the red, green, and blue values for the specified palette color numbers.

Example

```
TO SEE_COLORS
MAKE "A 0
MAKE "B 0
MAKE "C 0
LABEL "COL1
MAKE "COLOR SENTENCE :A :B
MAKE "COLOR SENTENCE :COLOR :C
SETPAL 1 :COLOR
MAKE "A :A + 1000/8
IF :A >1000 [GO "COL2]
GO "COL1
LABEL "COL2
MAKE "A 0
MAKE "COLOR SENTENCE :A :B
MAKE "COLOR SENTENCE :COLOR :C
SETPAL 1 :COLOR
MAKE "B :B + 1000/8
IF :B >1000 [GO "COL3]
GO "COL2
LABEL "COL3
MAKE "B 0
MAKE "COLOR SENTENCE :A :B
MAKE "COLOR SENTENCE :COLOR :C
SETPAL 1 :COLOR
MAKE "C :C + 1000/8
IF :C >1000 [GO "DONE]
GO "COL3
LABEL "DONE
MAKE "A 0
MAKE "B 0
MAKE "C 0
MAKE "COLOR SENTENCE :A :B
MAKE "COLOR SENTENCE :COLOR :C
SETPAL 1 :COLOR
END
```

SETPAN

Definition

Repositions the turtle's home position to match the input X and Y values. The default position is in the center of the screen.

Example

```
TO PAN_TURTLE
CS ST
MAKE "A 0
LABEL "LOOP
MAKE "B SENTENCE :A 0
SETPAN :B
```

```
MAKE "A :A + 5
IF :A > 200 [GO "NEXT]
GO LOOP
LABEL "NEXT
MAKE "B SENTENCE 0 :A
SETPAN :B
MAKE "A :A + 5
IF :A > 200 [GO "DONE]
GO "NEXT
LABEL "DONE
SETPAN [0 0]
END
```

SETPC

Definition

Changes the color, width, and pattern of the lines that the turtle draws in the Graphics Display window. Does not affect lines already in the window. To see the new color, you need to draw new lines.

Example

```
TO STAR
CS HT
MAKE "A 0
LABEL "LOOP
SETH RANDOM 360
SETPC RANDOM 4
FD RANDOM 100 HOME
MAKE "A :A + 1
IF :A > 30 [OUTPUT "DONE!]
GO "LOOP
END
```

SETPOS

Definition

Positions the turtle at the specified X and Y coordinates in the Graphics Display window.

Example

```
TO POS_TURT
CS PU ST
MAKE "X 0
LABEL "LOOP
MAKE "A RANDOM 150
MAKE "POSITION :A RANDOM 150
SETPOS :POSITION
MAKE "X :X + 1
IF :X > 50 [GO "DONE]
```

```
GO "LOOP
LABEL "DONE
END
```

SETSCRUNCH

Definition

Scales the Graphics Display window Y coordinate values to the specified scrunch value.

Example

```
TO SEE_SCRUNCH
; SCRUNCH1
SETSCRUNCH 1
CS PD ST
MAKE "X 0
LABEL "LOOP
MAKE "A RANDOM 150
MAKE "POSITION :A RANDOM 150
SETPOS :POSITION
MAKE "X :X + 1
IF  :X > 50 [GO "DONE]
GO "LOOP
LABEL "DONE
; SCRUNCH2
SETSCRUNCH 2
CS PD ST
MAKE "X 0
LABEL "LOOP2
MAKE "A RANDOM 150
MAKE "POSITION :A RANDOM 150
SETPOS :POSITION
MAKE "X :X + 1
IF  :X > 50 [GO "DONE2]
GO "LOOP2
LABEL "DONE2
END
```

SETTEXT

Definition

Changes the text style.

Example

```
TO SEE_TEXT_STYLES
MAKE "A 0
LABEL "LOOP
SETTEXT :A
PRINT [THE QUICK BROWN FOX]
```

```
PRINT CHAR 32
MAKE "A :A + 1
IF :A > 32 [GO "DONE]
GO "LOOP
LABEL "DONE
END
```

SETX

Definition

Positions the turtle at the specified X coordinate in the Graphics Display window.

SETY

Definition

Positions the turtle at the specified Y coordinate in the Graphics Display window.

SETZOOM

Definition

Scales the X and Y coordinate values to the specified values. Magnifies or reduces new images as they are drawn. Does not affect images already in the Graphics Display window.

Example

```
TO SEE_ZOOM
; ZOOM1
SETZOOM 1
CS PD ST
MAKE "X 0
LABEL "LOOP
MAKE "A RANDOM 150
MAKE "POSITION :A RANDOM 150
SETPOS :POSITION
MAKE "X :X + 1
IF  :X > 50 [GO "DONE]
GO "LOOP
LABEL "DONE
; ZOOM2
SETZOOM 2
CS PD ST
MAKE "X 0
LABEL "LOOP2
MAKE "A RANDOM 150
MAKE "POSITION :A RANDOM 150
SETPOS :POSITION
```

```
MAKE "X :X + 1
IF  :X > 50 [GO "DONE2]
GO "LOOP2
LABEL "DONE2
END
```

SHOW

Definition

Puts the specified text in the LOGO Dialog window. SHOW always moves the text cursor to the beginning of the next line after printing a line of text.

Example

```
TO SAY_HELLO
PRINT [ENTER YOUR NAME]
MAKE "A READLIST
PRINT [HELLO THERE]
SHOW :A
END

ENTER YOUR NAME
JOHN
HELLO THERE
[JOHN]
```

SHOWTURTLE (ST)

Definition

Makes the turtle reappear.

SHUFFLE

Definition

Rearranges the items in a list so they follow a pseudorandom order.

Example

```
TO MIX-UP
MAKE "A [1 2 3 4 5 6 7 8 9]
PRINT :A
MAKE "B SHUFFLE :A
PRINT :B
END

[1 2 3 4 5 6 7 8 9]
[8 1 9 7 6 5 3 2 4]
```

SIN

Definition

Calculates the sine of a number.

Example

```
SIN 3
0.052336
```

SORT

Definition

Rearranges a list to follow an alphabetic or numeric order.

Example

```
PRINT :A
MAKE "B SHUFFLE :A
PRINT :B
MAKE "C SORT :B
PRINT :C
END

[1 2 3 4 5 6 7 8 9]
[8 1 9 7 6 5 3 2 4]
[1 2 3 4 5 6 7 8 9]
```

SQRT

Definition

Calculates the square root of a number.

Example

```
SQRT 7
2.645751
```

STOP

Definition

Makes the procedure that is running stop at the designated line. Similar to PAUSE but unrecoverable with CO.

SUM

Definition

Adds numbers.

Example

```
SUM 4 5
9
```

TAN

Definition

Calculates the tangent of a number.

Example

```
TAN 70
2.747477
```

THROW

Definition

Jumps to a line label or external procedure specified in a CATCH command.

TO

Definition

Defines a procedure.

Example

```
TO TRACK
LABEL "LOOP
SETH TOWARDS MOUSE
GO "LOOP
END
```

TOWARDS

Definition

Rotates the turtle so it points at a specified X and Y coordinate.

Example

```
TURTLEFACTS
[0 0 157.166018 PD 2 TRUE]
```

TRACE

Definition

Causes the ST to display the names and values of all the procedures and variables called or generated by a procedure as they are executed.

TURTLEFACTS (TF)

Definition

Displays the current settings of the turtle. The data is

X, Y, H, PS, PC, V

where X and Y are the turtle's current position, H is the turtle's heading, PS is the pen state (PU, PD, PX), PC is the pen color, and V is visible/invisible.

TURTLETEXT (TT)

Definition

Prints the specified text in the Graphics Display window at the turtle.

Example

```
TT [ENTER YOUR NAME]
MAKE "A READLIST
TT [HELLO THERE]
TT :A
END

ENTER YOUR NAME
HELLO THERE
JOHN
```

TYPE

Definition

Puts the specified text in the LOGO Dialog window. TYPE does not move the cursor to the beginning of the next line after printing.

Example

```
PRINT [ENTER YOUR NAME]
MAKE "A READLIST
TYPE [HELLO THERE]
TYPE CHAR 32 TYPE :A
END

ENTER YOUR NAME
JOHN
HELLO THERE JOHN
```

UNBURY

Definition

Allows a package of procedures to be edited (*see also:* BURY, PACKAGE).

UPPERCASE

Definition

Converts all of the alphabetic characters of a string into uppercase letters.

Example

```
MAKE "A [hello there]
PRINT :A
PRINT UPPERCASE :A
HELLO THERE
```

WATCH

Definition

Causes the ST to display the operations and variable values generated by a procedure as it is executed.

WHERE

Definition

Returns the item number.

Example

```
MAKE "A [THE QUICK BROWN FOX]
MEMBERP BROWN :A
TRUE
WHERE
3
```

WINDOW

Definition

Disables a WRAP or FENCE command. Returns the Graphics Display window to its default mode.

WORD

Definition

Creates a string that contains the specified item.

Example

```
MAKE "A "HELLO
MAKE "B "THERE
MAKE "C WORD :A :B
PRINT :A :B :C
HELLO
THERE
HELLOTHERE
```

WRAP

Definition

Causes the turtle to continue drawing at the other side of the Graphics Display window when it leaves the window.

XCOR

Definition

Returns the horizontal (X) coordinate of the turtle's present location in the Graphics Display window.

YCOR

Definition

Returns the vertical (Y) coordinate of the turtle's present location in the Graphics Display window.

APPENDIX

Characters and Their ASCII Codes A

The Atari ST has the ability to display 512 different characters. One set of 256 characters uses an 8×8 matrix; the other set of 256 characters uses a 16×8 matrix. Figures A-1 and A-2 show all of the ST characters and their associated ASCII values. Use these in procedures that use the CHAR and ASCII primitives.

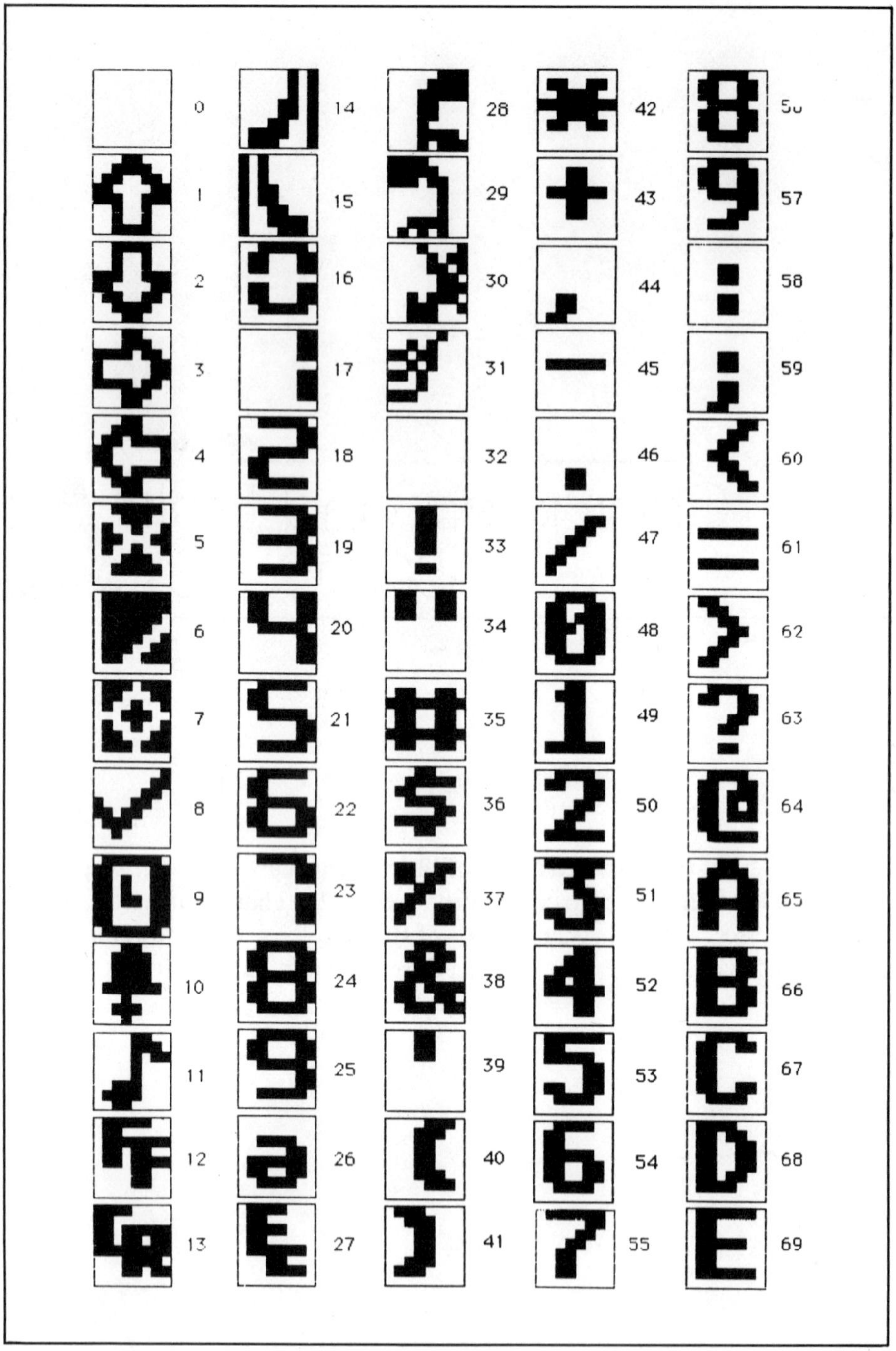

FIGURE A-1. The 8×8 character set

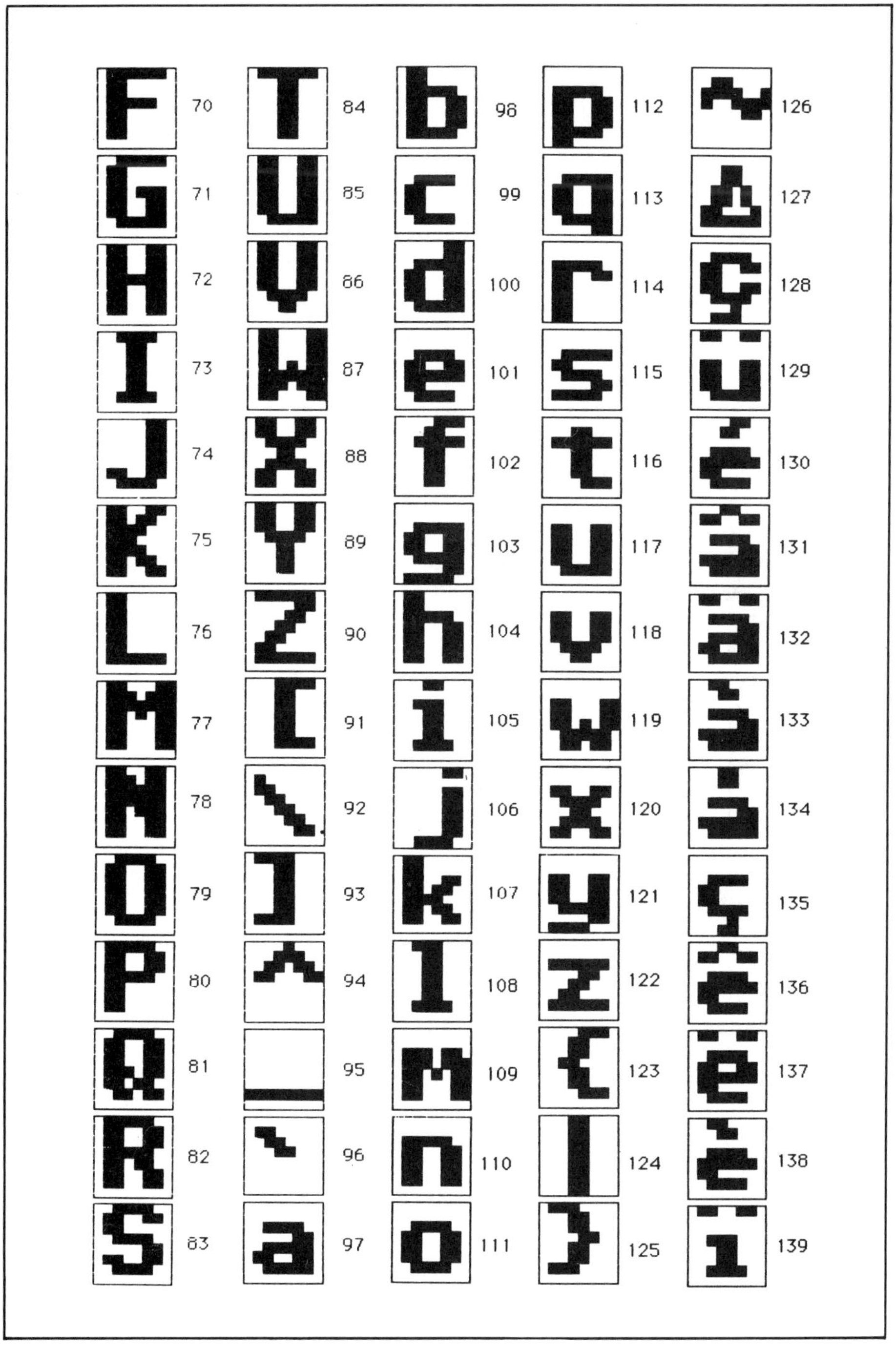

FIGURE A-1. The 8×8 character set (*continued*)

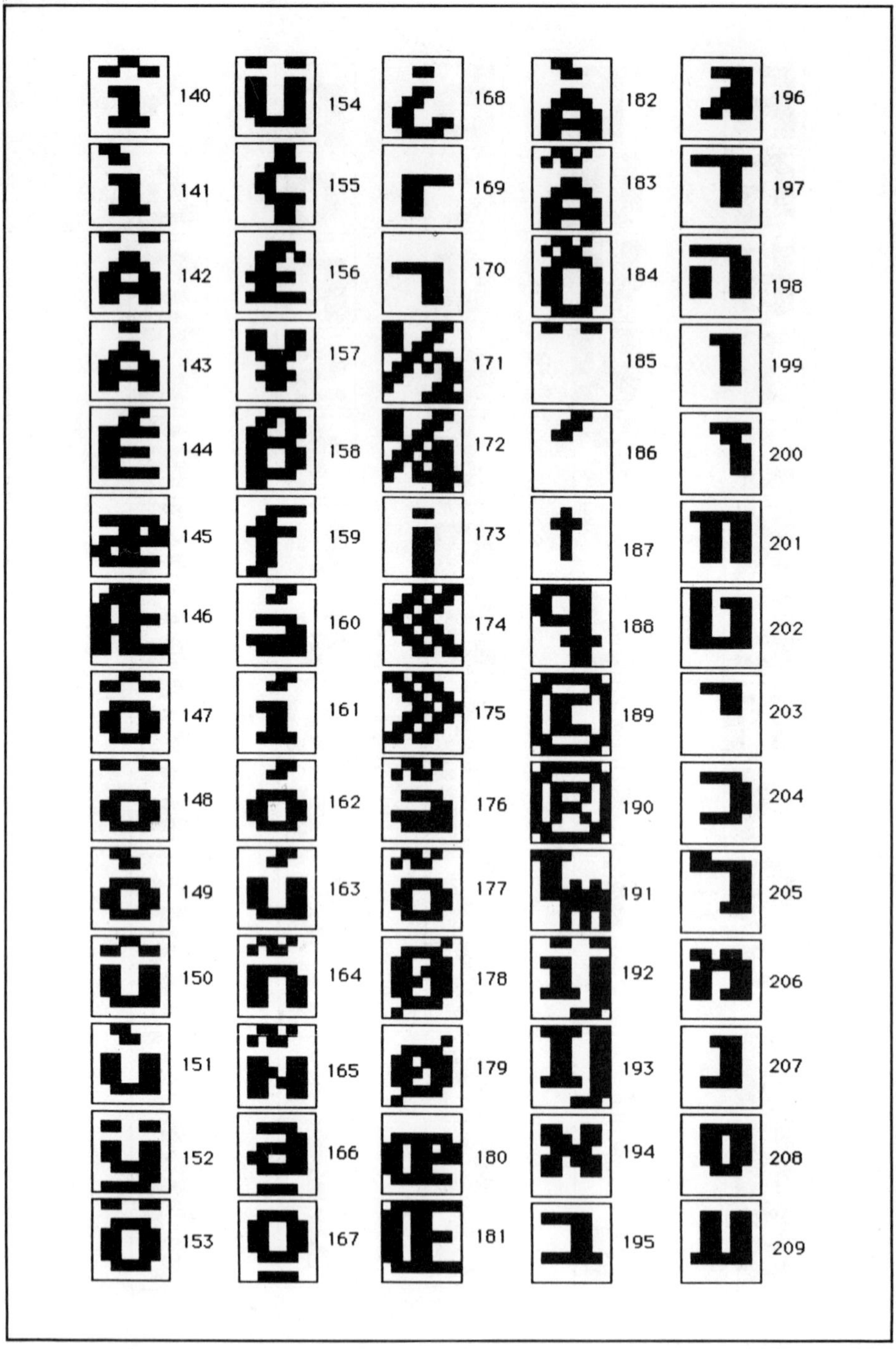

FIGURE A-1. The 8×8 character set (*continued*)

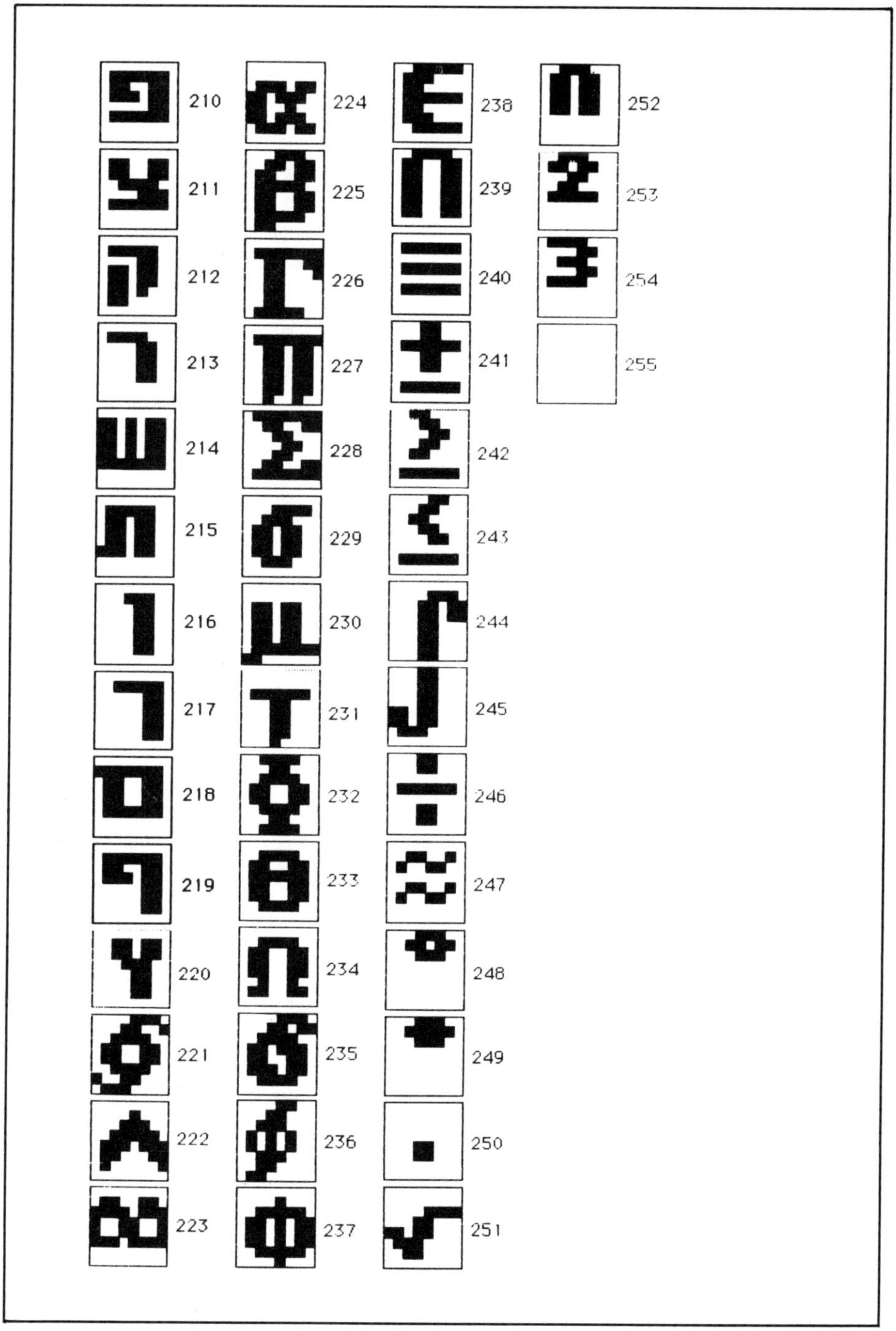

FIGURE A-1. The 8×8 character set (*continued*)

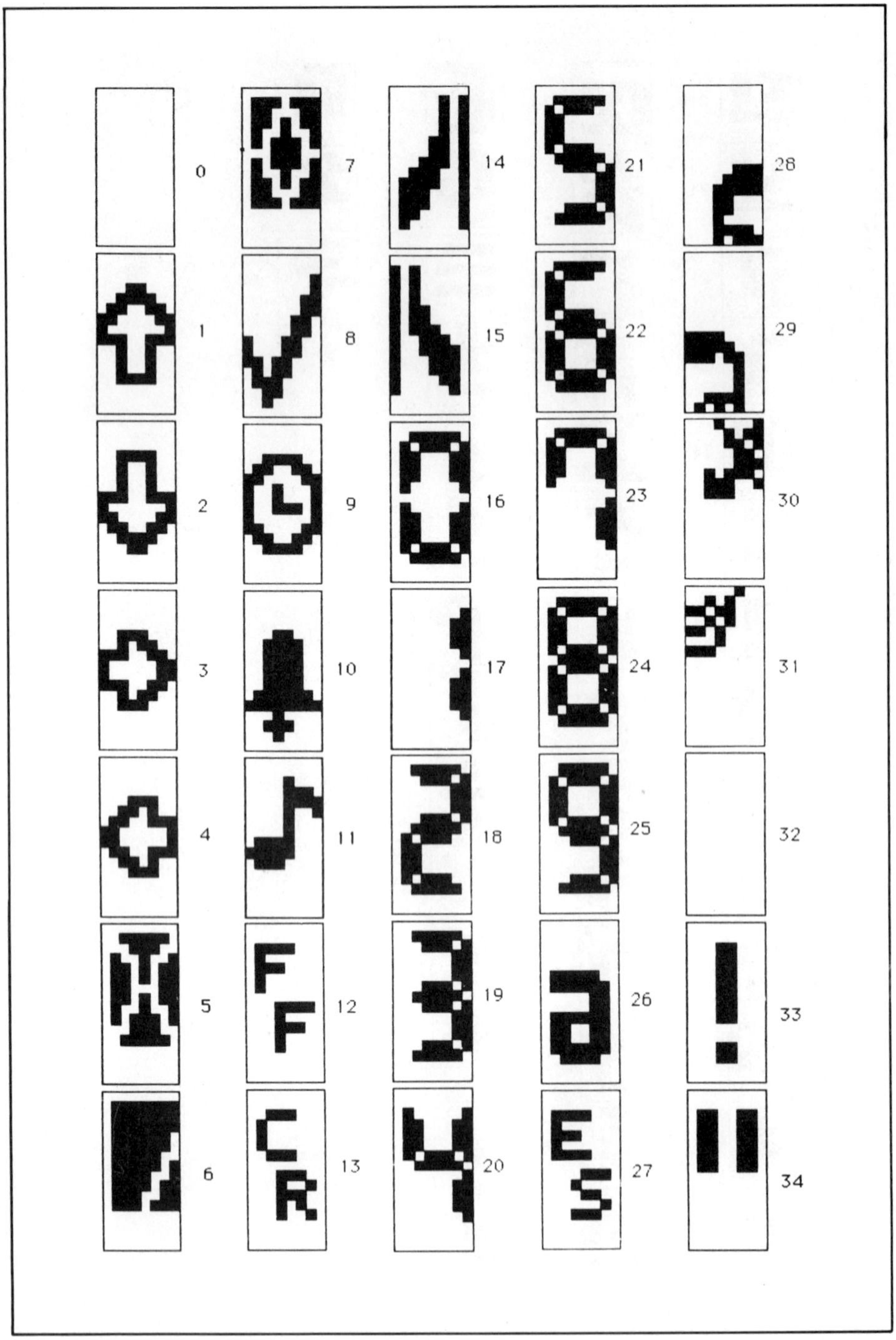

FIGURE A-2. The 8×16 character set

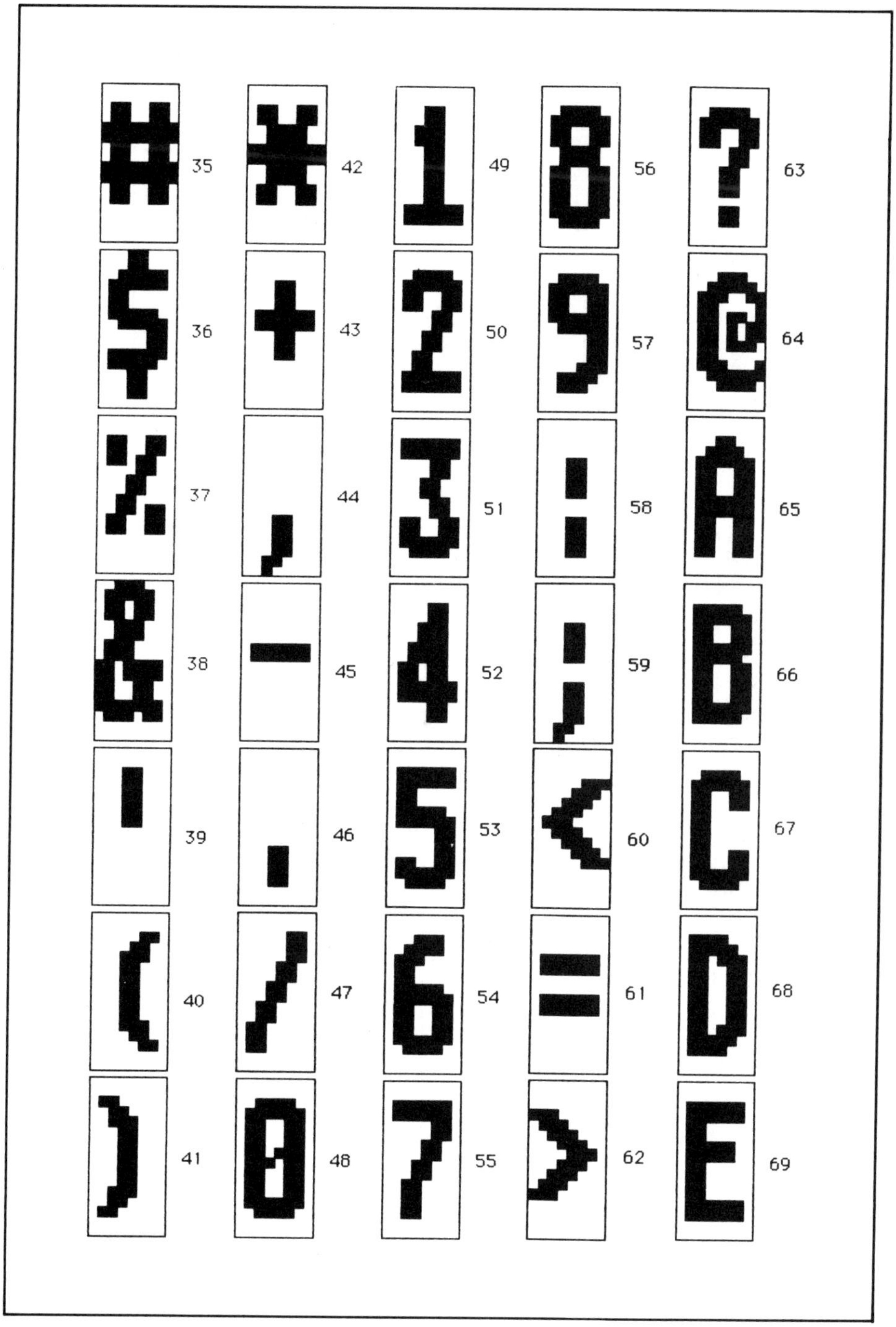

FIGURE A-2. The 8×16 character set (*continued*)

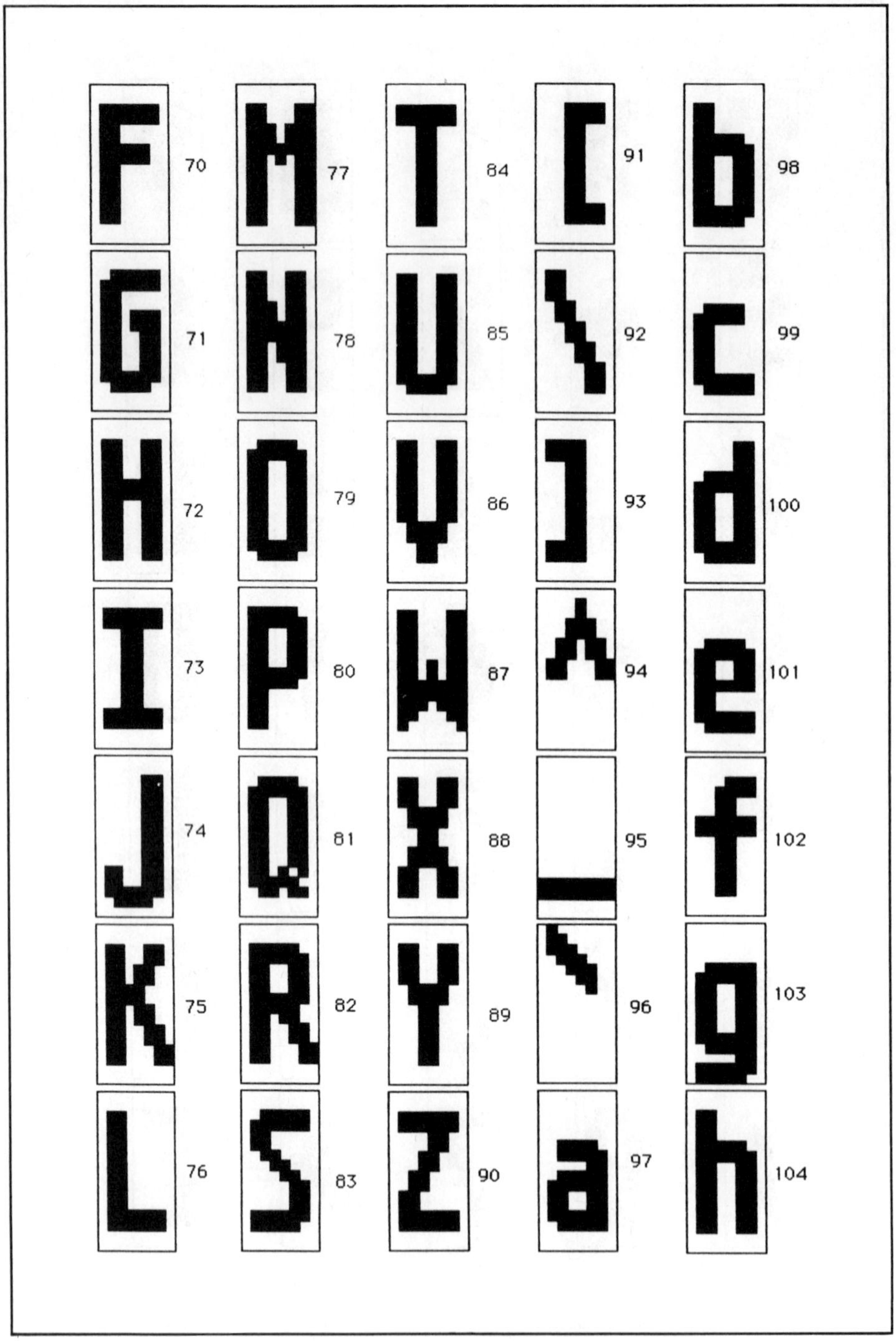

FIGURE A-2. The 8×16 character set (*continued*)

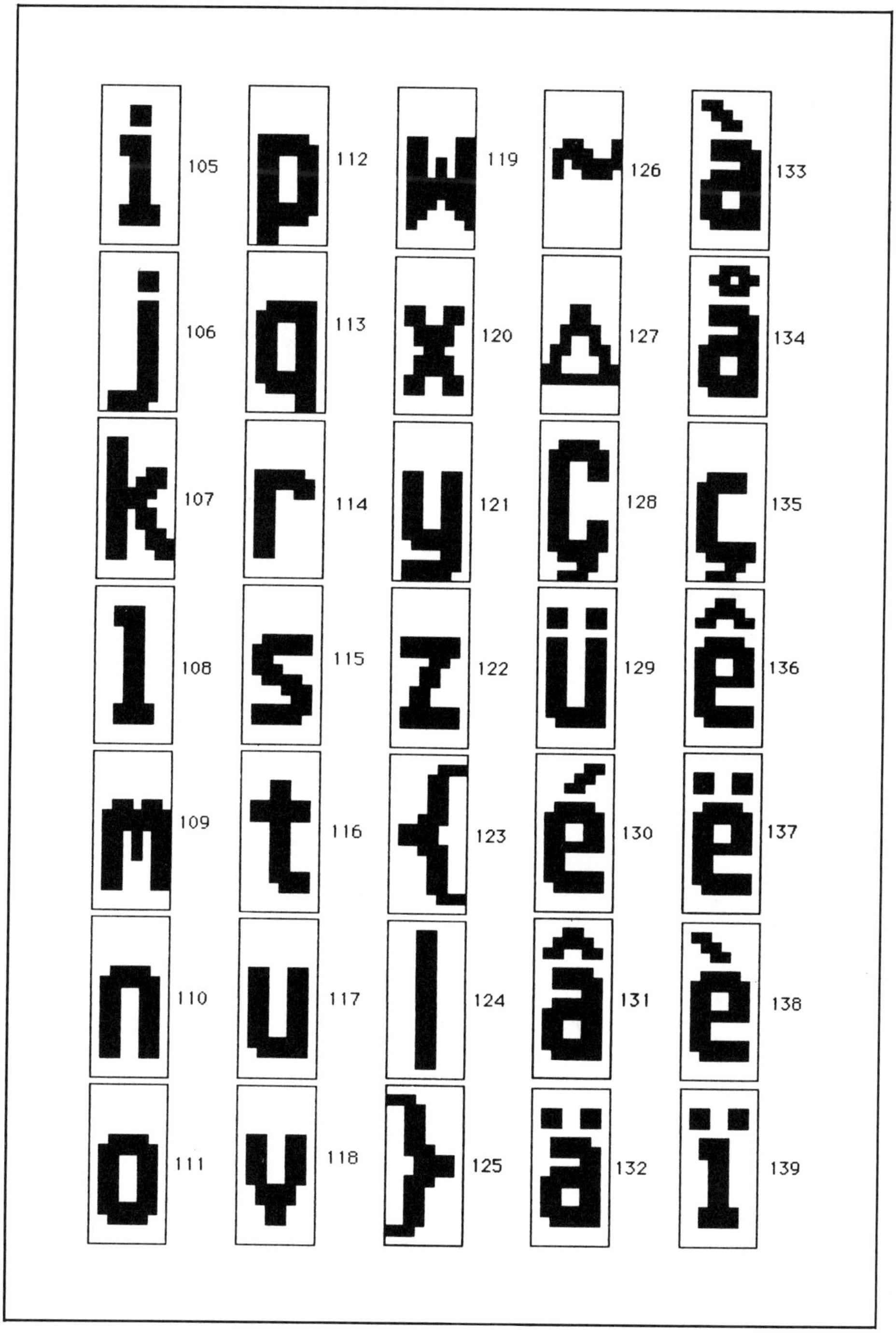

FIGURE A-2. The 8×16 character set (*continued*)

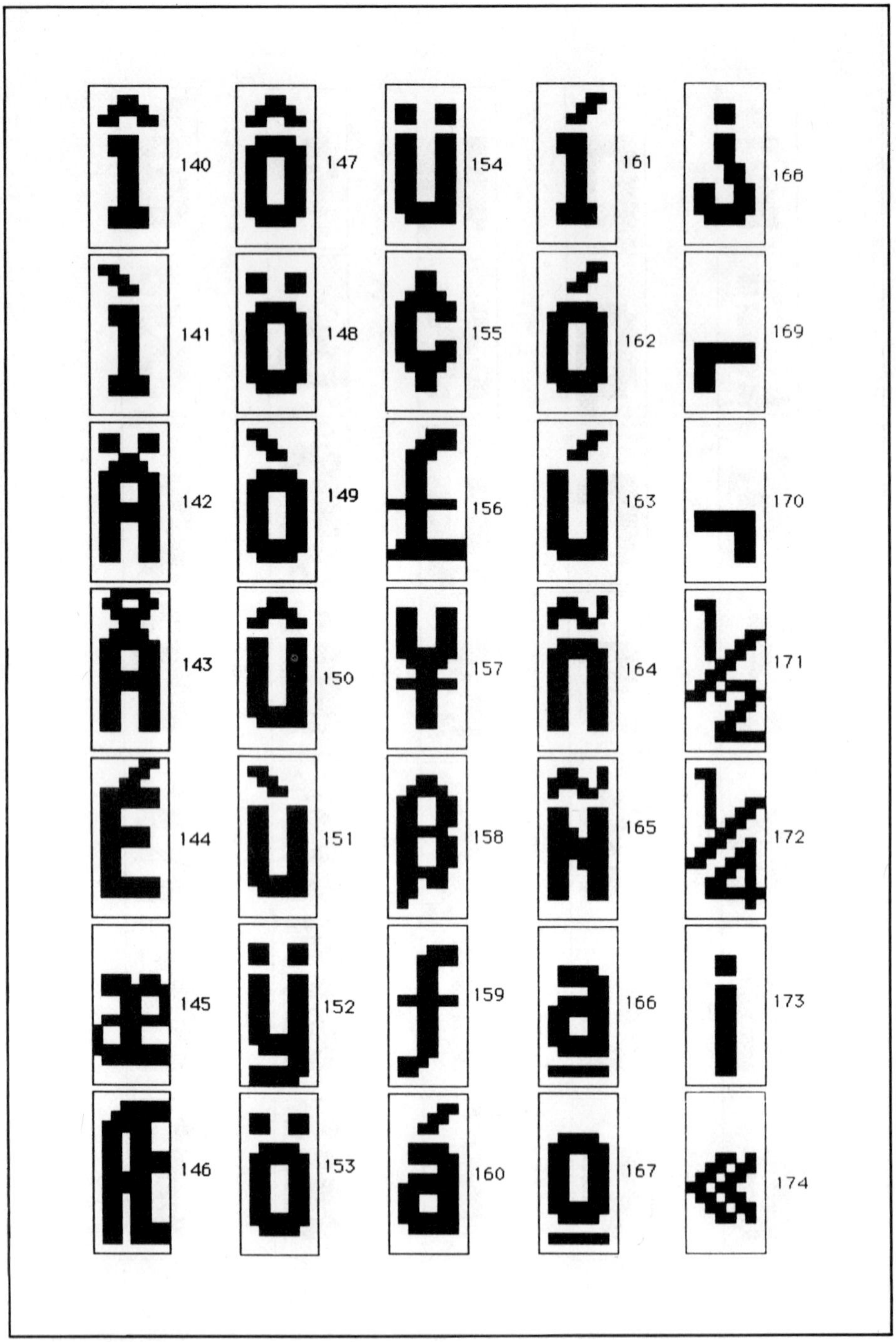

FIGURE A-2. The 8×16 character set (*continued*)

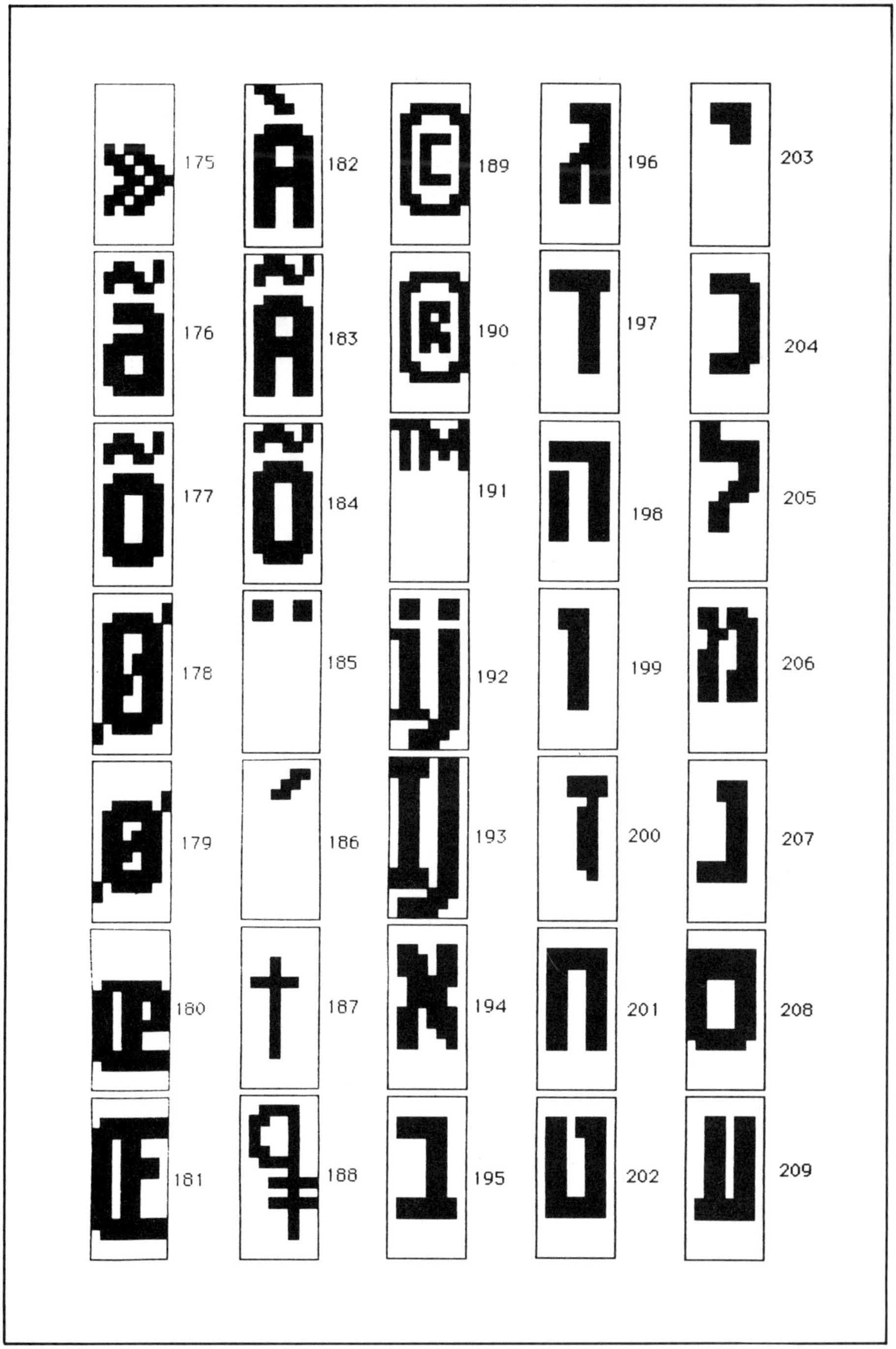

FIGURE A-2. The 8×16 character set (*continued*)

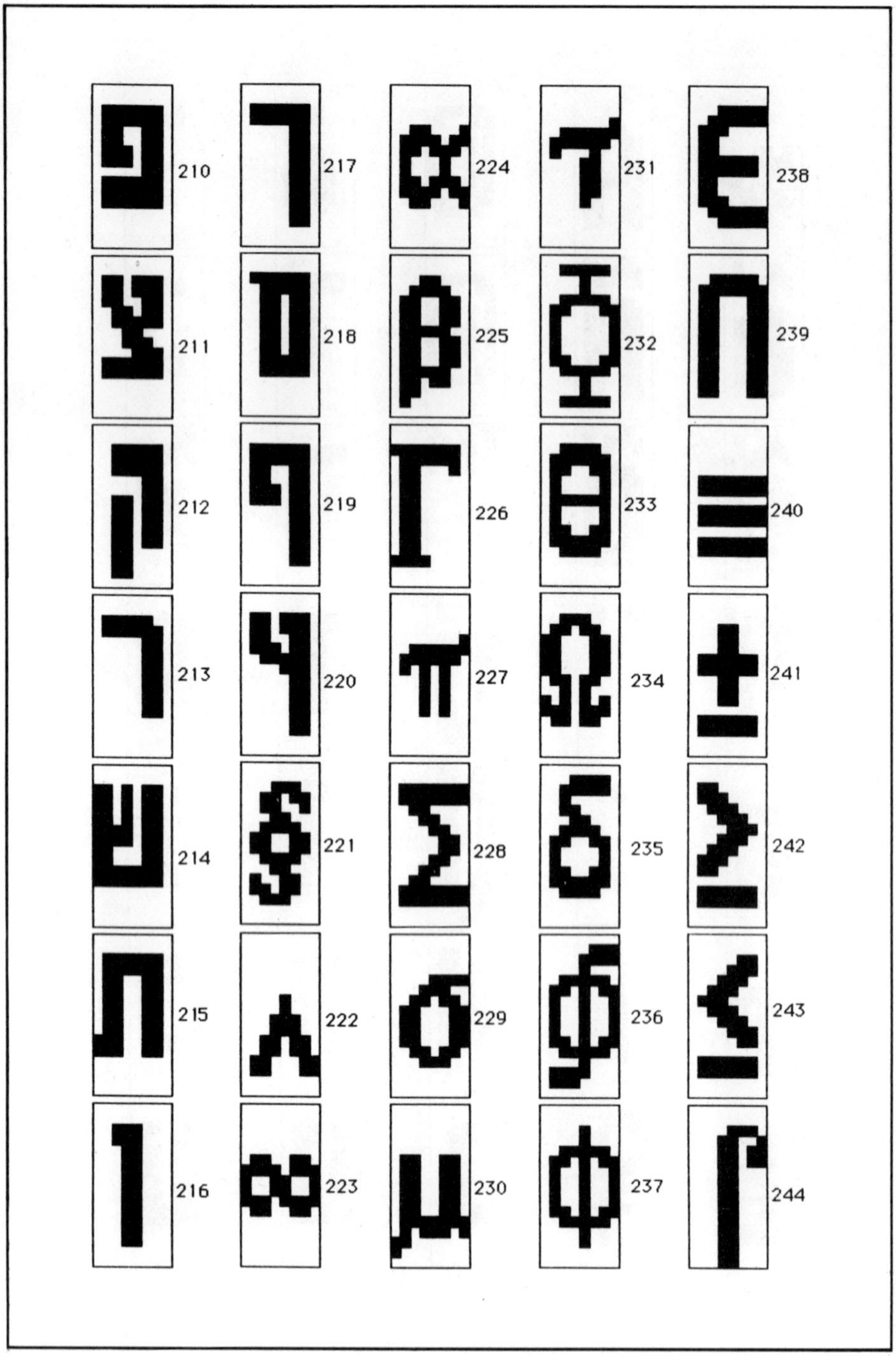

FIGURE A-2. The 8×16 character set (*continued*)

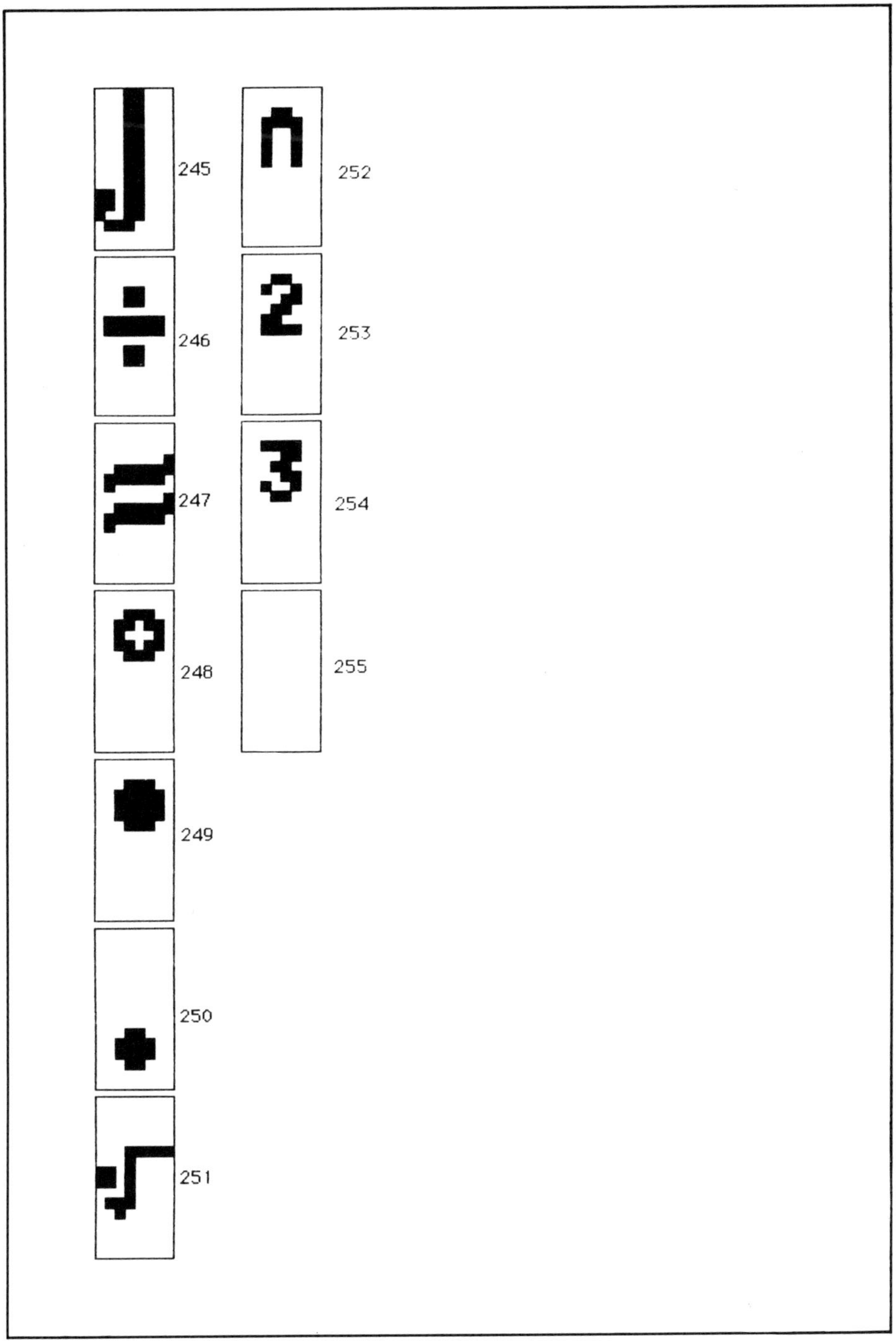

FIGURE A-2. The 8×16 character set (*continued*)

APPENDIX

Editing Commands B

In addition to the labeled editing controls on the keyboard (the arrow keys, the backspace key, HOME, and so on), ST LOGO has many special editing commands that you can use to edit your procedures.

- ^A — Positions the cursor at the beginning of the current line.
- ^B — Moves the cursor one character to the left without deleting the characters it moves over (similar to the left-arrow key).
- ^E — Positions the cursor at the right end of the current line.
- ^F — Moves the cursor one character to the right without deleting the characters it moves over (similar to the right-arrow key).
- ^H — Erases the character directly to the left of the cursor and moves the cursor one character position to the left (similar to the DELETE key).
- ^I — Performs the same function as the TAB key. It moves the cursor (and any text that is to the right of the cursor) to the next tab position to the right.

- ^K—Deletes all of the characters between the cursor and the end of the current line.
- ^N—Moves the cursor one row down without deleting the characters it moves over (similar to the down-arrow key).
- ^O—Moves all of the text to the right of the cursor down to the next line. It also moves any other text in the editing window down a row, and it leaves the cursor in its current position.
- ^P—Moves the cursor one row up without deleting the characters it moves over (similar to the up-arrow key).
- ^R—Positions the cursor at the top of text in the window (similar to the HOME key).
- ^U—Moves the text up the height of the current window, placing the last shown line of text at the top of the window. It also puts the cursor at the beginning of that line.
- ^V—Moves the text down the height of the current window, placing the first shown line of text at the bottom of the window. It also puts the cursor at the beginning of that line.
- ^X—Positions the cursor at the bottom of text in the Edit window (opposite of the HOME key).

APPENDIX

C Errors and Alerts

Whenever you operate ST LOGO, it will constantly check on the syntax of what you type. If you enter something that it cannot decipher, ST LOGO will stop whatever it is doing and display a small window that contains an error or alert message. While the meanings of these messages are often obvious, on some occasions they can be cryptic. This appendix explains the meaning of each of the ST LOGO error messages and alerts.

Number too big

You have entered a number that is larger than the maximum size allowed by ST LOGO, or the result of one of your calculations is larger than the maximum size allowed by ST LOGO.

No file selected

You are attempting a file operation, but you have not entered a file name.

----- is a primitive

You are attempting to name a procedure with a name that is reserved for an existing primitive.

Can't find LABEL -----

You have referenced a label name in your procedure (such as GO "labelname) but you have not defined that label with a LABEL statement. This is often encountered if you forget to precede the label name with a quotation mark.

I'm having trouble with the disk

This can result from a number of conditions, such as:

- A bad or damaged disk
- A bad connection to the disk drive
- The disk drives' power cable is not connected.

Disk is full

You have filled the disk with as many files as it can hold.

Can't divide by zero

You are attempting to divide by zero. Check your calculations and make sure that you are not using an undefined (or previously defined) variable.

File already exists

You are attempting to save a file by using a name that is assigned to an existing file. If you wish to replace the existing file, you must delete it before you save the new file.

File not found

You have attempted to open or load a file that is not on the disk.

Can't find CATCH for -----

You have assigned a CATCH statement, but you have not defined the label or procedure name for CATCH.

I'm out of space

You have used all of the available memory space.

----- is not true or false

You have asked LOGO to evaluate an expression as either true or false, and it is neither.

Not enough inputs to -----

The procedure you are using requires more parameters than you have assigned.

Turtle out of bounds

You have entered a statement that will move the turtle outside of the established FENCE.

I don't know how to-----

You are asking LOGO to execute a procedure that has not been defined.

----- has no value

You are using a variable that has not been defined.

I don't know what to do with -----

You have performed an operation but have not told LOGO what to do with the results.

Disk is write-protected

You are attempting to save to a disk that is physically write-protected. If you really want to write to the disk, move the write-protect tab up.

----- doesn't like ----- as input

You are attempting to use a parameter that does not work with the given procedure or primitive.

----- didn't output to -----

You are attempting to assign a value to a parameter that does not work with the given procedure or primitive.

The word is too long

You are attempting to create a word with too many characters.

I don't have enough buffer space

You have run out of available memory for the operation.

IF wants [ ]*'s around instructions*

You are attempting to branch to a procedure, but you have not delineated the instructions with brackets.

----- *isn't a parameter*

You are attempting to use a parameter that does not work with the given procedure or primitive.

No PAN with FENCE or WRAP

You have used a PAN command after previously using WRAP or FENCE.

Trademarks

The following names are trademarked products of the corresponding companies.

Atari®	Atari, Inc.
520-ST™	Atari, Inc.
SM124™	Atari, Inc.
SC1224™	Atari, Inc.
Centronics™	Data Computer Corporation
VT52®	Digital Equipment Corporation
QMS®	Quality Micro Systems
Smartwriter™	Quality Micro Systems

Index

A

B

C

D

E

F

G

H

I

J

K

L

M

N

O

P